Wildflowers of Garland Ranch

A field guide to the wild flowers together with selected trees, shrubs, reeds, rushes and ferns of Garland Ranch, Carmel, California

By

Michael Mitchell and Rod M. Yeager, MD

First Printing 2011
Second Printing (Revised Edition) 2011
Third Printing (Revised) 2013

ISBN: 978-0-578-07859-5

The Photographs

All but two of the photographs are by one or other of the authors. All of the species illustrated have been photographed by them in Garland Ranch. Photography can however be an uncertain art and neither plants nor weather conditions (especially the wind) are necessarily cooperative. We have therefore used photographs taken in other locations where this gives a better view of a flower or some particular aspect that we are trying to illustrate.

We thank Jim McCammon for permission to use two of his photographs; the beautiful close up of the Fiesta Flower and the photograph providing a clear illustration of how the Shepherd's Purse got its name.

About the Authors

Michael Mitchell is a native Englishman who moved to Carmel Valley upon his retirement from a lifetime of legal practice in England and California. An enthusiastic photographer and nature lover, he has spent many happy hours photographing and then struggling to identify the local wild flowers. His struggles convinced him of the need for a guide such as this to enable others to spend more time enjoying and hopefully less time trying to identify the myriad flowers to be found in Garland Ranch. He is a volunteer naturalist with the Monterey Peninsula Regional Park District.

Rod M. Yeager, MD is a native of Louisiana and retired to Pebble Beach after many years of practice as a cardiovascular surgeon in Shreveport LA. His interest in hiking and wildflowers gradually took the place of an earlier passion for golf and was soon accompanied by a passion for photographing the many wildflowers that he saw on his hikes. He has accumulated an extensive collection of photographs many of which he has made available on his website (www.rodyeager.com) for the benefit of those (among whom his co-author would count himself) lacking the benefit of his knowledge and experience.

Preface to the Revised Edition

In the original edition of this book, we noted that Garland Ranch was home to over 350 flowering plants, shrubs and trees. We should have said "over 450"; including grasses, it is over 550 or about 25% of all of the flowering plants to be found in the whole of Monterey County. Many of the flowers that we have found and photographed for the first time during the course of this year cry out for inclusion in the book.

In the original edition, we mentioned the fact that the Jepson Manual, the ultimate reference work for anyone interested in the flora of California, was in the process of revision. We understand that it is due to be published very early in 2012; in the meantime, an online version is available which has made it possible for us to learn what changes in family, genus and species are being proposed and will be found in the new edition.

Since many of these changes are already common currency in the botanical world and the remainder soon will be, it seemed appropriate to take this opportunity of updating the families and scientific names of the plants in this book. We have included a section following our discussion of Scientific Names and Taxonomy on page viii of the Introduction listing those plants where either the family or the genus has changed. In the body of the book, the family or scientific name is followed by an asterisk to indicate where there has been a change.

For the less scientifically minded, the good news is that the common names have not changed. The plants themselves have definitely not changed. Our understanding of them may have become more sophisticated but our ability to enjoy and appreciate them remains untouched. We may however, from time to time, recall the wry humor of Corky Matthews' comment to one of the authors that, as time passes, she has become more and more convinced that there is in fact only one species of plant - of infinite variety.

Michael Mitchell
Rod M. Yeager MD

Carmel, November 2011

Preface to the First Edition

The 3,464 acres of Garland Ranch in Carmel Valley are home to over 350 flowering plants, shrubs and trees but there is no readily accessible guide that enables someone without specialist botanical knowledge to identify them.

This book is offered to those who delight in the beauty and variety of the wildflowers to be found in Garland Ranch (many of which will be found in many other parts of the Monterey Peninsula) and who would like to know what it is they are looking at, who perhaps want to learn a little more about the flowers or who would simply like to have a reminder of the beauty that they experienced when visiting the park.

We have included all but a very few of the flowers that we have seen and photographed at Garland Ranch and have included as well a number of shrubs, a few trees and a selection of the more common reeds, rushes and ferns that will be found in Garland Ranch.

We have tried very hard to avoid technical terms. The bewildering variety of plants and the complexity of their different structures has spawned an extensive technical language which is almost completely impenetrable to anyone who is neither a botanical specialist nor a dedicated amateur. Some terms cannot however be avoided and we have tried to explain and illustrate these in the introduction as well as including a short glossary inside the front cover.

Identifying plants from photographs can be an uncertain business. Sometimes it is easy, at other times it is necessary to look at the structure of the plant in order to identify it with confidence. A book such as this cannot provide a definitive guide but we hope that it will take the layman as far as he or she wishes to go and that it will not offend the specialist by its necessarily brief and superficial treatment of the finer points of botanical anatomy.

Michael Mitchell
Rod M. Yeager MD

Carmel, January 2011

www.montereywildflowers.com

The authors have recently put out this website which covers close to 1,000 species of Wildflowers, Trees, Shrubs and Ferns to be found in the Monterey Peninsula. Some species found in Garland Ranch but not (for reasons of space) included in this book are covered by the website as well as many species not found in Garland Ranch at all.

Acknowledgements

First and foremost we should like to thank Corky Matthews for her encouragement and assistance but above all for the inspiration provided by her enthusiasm for and huge knowledge of the wildflowers of Monterey County. We should also like to thank the many individuals with whom we have hiked and searched for wildflowers and without whose knowledge and experience our task would have been far harder. While it is invidious to single out any one individual, it would be wrong not to mention Gordon Williams who has been involved with local wildflowers since before many of us were born and shows every sign of continuing until long after we have all gone. We should also like to thank John Castagna for his advice and invaluable practical assistance on some of the technical aspects of producing a book such as this. Lastly, but certainly not least, we should like to thank our wives, Sharon and Elizabeth, who have at different times inspired and tolerated an interest which all too often extends a short hike into a lengthy expedition. Without all of them, this book would probably never have seen the light of day.

Introduction

Garland Ranch

Garland Ranch is a regional park in Carmel Valley, part of the Monterey Peninsula in Northern California, managed by the Monterey Peninsula Regional Park District. It comprises 3,464 acres at the northern end of the Santa Lucia mountain range with the Carmel River running along some of its northern boundary. Its 50 miles of hiking trails allow the visitor to explore a diverse range of habitats, from the riparian, along the Carmel River and the creeks that flow into it, to a flood plain rising, sometimes steeply, through lowland oak woodlands and redwoods to sage brush and chaparral before reaching the ridge lines, at between 1500 and 2000 feet, with their exposed grasslands and scrub.

From a human perspective, Garland Ranch enjoys an almost ideal combination of the coastal and inland microclimates. During the summer months the park will normally be shrouded in the coastal fog during the nights and early mornings but will enjoy warm sunshine during much of the day without ever getting too hot. The wooded lower areas provide plenty of shade for those flowers, particularly the early spring flowers, that need it. The more exposed higher areas provide abundant sunshine for the meadow flowers and for the summer and fall flowers that thrive in hotter and dryer conditions.

Garland Ranch is home to over 450 species of flowering plants, flowers, shrubs and trees; over 550 if one includes grasses. The spring and early summer see the greatest abundance of flowers. An observant hiker who goes through both the woodland areas and chaparral to the ridges may expect to see close to 100 species in a day. By the late fall, the number will have dropped substantially but there is almost no time of the year when there are not interesting flowers to see if one keeps one's eyes open.

The Arrangement of this Book

There are many ways to organize a book such as this. We have chosen to group plants first by the color of their flowers or, in some cases where the flowers may appear in a variety of colors (such as the Scarlet Pimpernel), by their most typical color. The choice of color category (especially with pale purple to purplish-pink flowers) is unavoidably subjective. The species are then (with a few exceptions) arranged by families (taking the Latin (or, more accurately, scientific) names of the families in alphabetical order) and then by genus (also in Latin alphabetical order). In this edition we have moved the rushes and reeds to the end of the green section and added at the end four brown (to match the earth) pages of "belly" flowers, i.e. very low growing plants with tiny flowers barely discernible to the naked eye.

Many wildflowers have more than one common name. The same common name may be used by several plants, sometimes of different species. For these (and other) reasons, it makes for more consistency if the arrangement follows the unique scientific names. These names have two components, the genus (the branch of the family to which the plant belongs) and the species (the particular individual member of that branch). In some cases there are subspecies or varieties. We have tried to identify these where possible but recognise that this can be an uncertain business - and not only because even expert botanists are not always in agreement.

Each page contains one or more photographs of the plant, generally trying to show different aspects of the plant so as to assist in its identification. There is an indication of the typical blooming season of the plant, the height of the plant, the size of its flower, its region of origin, if the plant is not native to California, and finally its "life-form"; e.g. whether is an annual, perennial or a shrub (see p. v below for an explanation of the term "life-form"). These indicators should be seen as guides rather than firm rules; there will frequently be exceptions, flowers that are larger or smaller than average, plants that are larger than normal and flowers that are to be found in bloom either before or after the normal flowering season.

Identification of Flowers

The trained botanist will 'key out' a plant, identifying particular features of its structure and appearance so as to identify first the family, then the genus and finally the species or subspecies. Because this book is not aimed at the trained botanist, it makes no attempt to follow this approach. Some elements of a plant's structure are however relevant when it comes to differentiating flowers that may at first sight be very similar and we do try to mention these elements so far as space permits.

For the layman, color is perhaps the first and most obvious starting point, but even this is not wholly reliable since there are a number of flowers (such as Scarlet Pimpernel, Elegant Clarkia or Padre's Shooting Star) where the same species may be found in several colors. Albino specimens also may be found in a number of species.

Petals are often cited as a prime indicator. Sometimes they are, for example most members of the Brassicaceae (Mustard) family have four petals, as do all of the Clarkias. In other cases, plants may have a variable number of petals (such as the Star Flower which may have between 5 and 8). Then, of course, there are the members of the Asteraceae (Sunflower) family which can have a widely varying number of what look like petals but are in fact separate 'ray flowers', each of which is an individual flower with reproductive organs of its own.

Where the flowers appear identical, it is often necessary to look at a plant's leaves. Good examples of this are the two blue Larkspurs found at Garland Ranch; their flowers are virtually identical, but their leaves are quite different. The same is true of the Lomatiums, of some of the Lupines, the Clovers and a number of other plants.

In other cases one has to look at a plant's fruit. At first glance, the members of a particular genus may look very similar but there can be subtle differences in their fruits that allows for a more certain identification.

Some understanding of a plant's structure is helpful and the selection of photographs on pp. xiv and xv is designed to illustrate some basic structural features and some of the technical terms to be found in this book.

The Structure of Plants

It is beyond the scope of this book to do more than illustrate a few of the more obvious features that will readily be visible with the naked eye (sometimes with the aid of a hand lens).

Specific attention should however be drawn to the Asteraceae which vary enormously in their appearance. Some (like the Daisies) may have ray flowers and disk flowers (sometimes in large numbers), some may have just disk flowers (like the Everlastings) and others (like the Dandelions and their relatives) have no disk flowers but only ligules which are like ray flowers except that they have 5 lobes rather than 3 and are bisexual and therefore capable of reproduction. Ray flowers are either sterile or pistillate (female) and therefore not capable of reproduction which is why one will never find an inflorescence with ray flowers alone, they are always accompanied by disk flowers. Close attention to the detail is amply rewarded.

A word should also be said about bracts and involucrae. With some species, the presence of a bract or involucre is critical to its precise identification. With clovers, for instance, noting whether or not the species has an involucre by itself halves the number of potential candidates. Bracts can easily be mistaken for a leaf, a sepal or even (e.g. with the Indian Paintbrushes) as part of the flower. An awareness of these two features of a plant's structure is helpful when trying to refine one's identification skills.

Some explanation of the term "Life-form" may be helpful. This derives from a system first proposed by a Danish botanist called Christen Raunkiaer in 1904, though much modified and elaborated since. The idea was to categorise plants by where their growth-points (perennating buds) appear in adverse growing conditions (e.g. winter or drought). Some plants project themselves into the air on stems with buds more than 25 cms above the soil (e.g. trees and shrubs). Some are similar but with the buds closer to the soil. Others have buds on or near the surface of the soil and others have their buds under the ground or in water. As a general rule, the closer to the surface the buds are to be found, the more tolerant of adverse conditions the plant will prove to be. Annuals form a separate group, relying on seeds, the ability of which to germinate may be dependent on specific conditions such as the heat generated by a fire (for the fire followers) or heavy rainfall (for certain desert plants). This approach offers insights into how groups of plants fit into different ecosystems and how adaptive they may be to changes in climate. For our, simpler, purposes it enables us to distinguish annuals from the various groups of perennial plants and so help us identify or locate certain plants of particular interest.

Leaves

It is frequently necessary to look at a plant's leaves in order to identify it. Leaves come in a bewildering variety of shapes, sizes and structures and there is an extensive terminology to describe sometimes subtle differences.

The first distinction is between simple and compound leaves. A simple leaf is not divided into separate leaflets. A compound leaf has three or more separate leaflets, either on a single stalk ('petiole') or further subdivided into separate groups on individual stems.

Leaves are often 'pinnate' in structure, with two groups of leaflets arranged on either side of a central axis. Ferns are a classic example of this structure. They may also be 'bipinnate' meaning that the individual leaflets also show a pinnate structure (the Wood Fern shows this structure very clearly).

Leaves, whether simple or not, frequently have 'lobes' (rounded segments which are more or less separated from the adjoining segment). Sometimes the segments are 'cut' (the Cut-leaved Geranium provides an extreme example of this).

The edges of leaves may be smooth, toothed or serrated (i.e. with the teeth pointing forward).

The books identify over 40 different shapes of leaves even before considering the shape of their tips. We have not tried to follow the technical terms for these shapes but have used instead a much simpler set of common terms which we hope will be a sufficient (though inevitably less accurate) guide.

Mention should be made of the way in which leaves attach to a plant's stem. The normal way is by a stalk (petiole). In some cases a leaf may be sessile (i.e. attached without any noticeable petiole). In other cases, it may be 'clasping' (i.e. with the base of the leaf partially or wholly surrounding the stem).

There are two principal kinds of leaves, basal and cauline. Basal leaves are those attached to the base of the plant's main stem. Cauline leaves are attached to the stem above its base.

Finally, it has to be accepted that leaves can be extraordinarily variable. From one plant to another of the same species, or even on the same plant, it is possible to find leaves that vary substantially in shape. Too much reliance should not be placed on the shape of a single leaf on any plant.

Indigenous peoples and their use of plants

We have listed below where particular plants which we believe may have been used by the indigenous people who lived in this part of the Monterey peninsula.

We make no claim to any specialised knowledge of this area and we are conscious that there is both much uncertainty and much debate about many aspects of what use was made of particular plants and by which particular group of the indigenous people.

Our aim is merely to indicate which plants are believed to have been used and how. We have deliberately not attempted to specify how something may have been used medicinally nor have we offered any recipes for the use of acorns or other plants.

It is thought that the local indigenous people spent part of the year by the Coast, taking advantage of the wide range of fish and shellfish that were available there, and part further inland, especially during the fall so as to take advantage of the greater number of oak trees whose acorns formed a material part of their diet. There is at least one bedrock mortar (used for grinding acorns) to be found at Garland Ranch to evidence the presence of the indigenous people.

They are thought to have made much use of controlled burning to keep down the understorey both to provide more grazing for animals that they might wish to hunt and to permit the active cultivation of particular plants which were of particular nutritional value.

Blackberry:	Food (also strawberries and gooseberries)
Brodiaea:	Medicinal uses, bulbs for food
Buckeye:	Seeds for food and used for stunning fish
Buckwheat:	Medicinal uses (leaves), seeds for food
Buttercups:	Seeds and roots for food
California Poppy:	Medicinal uses (stems and roots), leaves and flowers for food
Ceanothus:	Flowers and fruits used for soap, seeds for food
Checker Bloom:	Medicinal use; leaves for food
Chia:	Seeds for food and hydration
Clarkia:	Seeds for food
Coastal Live Oak:	Acorns for food
Coffeeberry:	Medicinal uses (berries)
Common Yarrow:	Medicinal uses
Coyote Brush:	Fire drills, medicinal uses (leaves)
Wild Cucumber:	Crafts (seeds used for beads), medicinal uses (seeds) and the leaves, crushed, for stunning fish
Douglas Iris:	Crafts, leaves used to make nets, snares and twine
Elderberry:	Wood for musical instruments (whistles and clappersticks), berries for food
Fremontia:	Stems for traps, snares, spears; medicinal uses
Goldenrod:	Medicinal uses (leaves)
Locoweed:	Medicinal uses, seeds for spice
Lupine:	Medicinal uses (seeds), early leaves for food
Madia:	Seeds for soap and food; flowers an antidote for poison oak
Madrone:	Berries for food
Manzanita:	Berries for food
Mariposa Lily:	Bulbs for food
Milkweeds:	Used to make cord and fish nets
Common Monkey Flower:	Medicinal uses (leaves), leaves and stems for food
Monterey Pine:	Pitch used as adhesive and sealant
Mugwort:	Stems used for basketry, medicinal uses (bark, leaves and stems), seeds and shoots for food
Miner's Lettuce:	Leaves for food
Mule Ears:	Shoots for food
Mule Fat:	Fire drills
Peppergrass:	Seeds for food
Poison Oak:	Dyeing, basket weaving
Rushes:	Used for basketry
Sagebrush:	Medicinal uses (leaves), seeds for food
Soap Plant:	Bulb for brushes and, crushed, for stunning fish, also for soap, glue and food
Toyon:	Berries for food (cooked)
White sage:	Ceremonial and medicinal uses
Yerba Buena:	Medicinal uses (infusion of leaves)

Scientific Names and Taxonomy

The scientific names used in the first edition of this book were those used in the two principal books covering Garland Ranch. These are The Jepson Manual Ed. James C Hickman *(Third printing) (University of California Press, 1996)* and An Illustrated Field Key to the Flowering Plants of Monterey County by Mary Ann Matthews *(California Native Plant Society, version 1.1, 2006).* The common names with one or two exceptions follow Matthews.

Because of the challenging nature of the technical vocabulary used in Jepson and in Matthews, we should mention the excellent book by James G and Melinda Woolf Harris - Plant Identification Terminology: an Illustrated Glossary *(2nd Edition, Spring Lake Publishing, 2001).*

The allocation of individual plants to a particular family or genus is something that has exercised botanists for many years. As more study is undertaken and more sophisticated tools (such as DNA analysis) become available, botanists are constantly reconsidering the classification of particular species.

The second and extensively revised edition of the Jepson Manual was published at the beginning of 2012 and reflects a large number of changes at the level of families, genera and species.

Among other changes, the Lily family is being split into a number of separate families, some families are being subsumed under other families (the Hydrophyllaceae, for example, will now be found with the Boraginaceae) and some families are being split up and reallocated (the Scrophulariaceae being the main example with almost all of its members being moved to other families, mainly the Plantaginaceae and Orobanchaceae).

The reader of this volume who wishes to pursue things in more depth is referred to Jepson and to Matthews.

This book now follows the changes reflected in the second edition of the Jepson Manual.

There follows a list of all of the plants in this book which have been the subject of either a change in family, genus or species. In the interests of space we have not included plants where the only change is the addition, omission or change of a subspecies classification. The list is in two parts. The first lists plants which have moved to a new family; these are listed in order of family name so that the family connections may be more apparent. The second lists plants whose genus or species attribution have changed; these are listed in alphabetical order by common name.

Note: "n/c" under "Old Scientific Name" in Part 1 indicates that there is no change in the genus or species; only in the family.

To save space, a "nominative" subspecies or variety (i.e. where the subspecies or variety name is the same as the species) is indicated by its initial letter only.

Part 1 - Changes in Family attribution with or without change in Genus or Species name

Common Name	Current Scientific Name	Old Scientific Name	Family (Latin)	Family (English)	Old Family (Latin)	Old Family (English)
Milkweed, Indian	Asclepias eriocarpa	n/c	Apocynaceae	Dogbane	Asclepiadaceae	Milkweed
Milkweed, Narrow-leaved	Asclepias fascicularis	n/c	Apocynaceae	Dogbane	Asclepidaceae	Milkweed
Elderberry, Blue	Sambucus nigra ssp. caerulea	Sambucus mexicana	Adoxaceae	Muskroot	Caprifoliaceae	Honeysuckle
Laurustinus	Viburnum tinus	n/c	Adoxaceae	Muskroot	Caprifoliaceae	Honeysuckle
Buckeye, California	Aesculus californica	n/c	Sapindaceae	Soapberry	Hipposcastanaceae	Buckeye
Whispering Bells	Emmenanthe penduliflora var. p.	n/c	Boraginaceae	Borage	Hydrophyllaceae	Waterleaf
Phacelia, Great Valley	Phacelia ciliata	n/c	Boraginaceae	Borage	Hydrophyllaceae	Waterleaf
Phacelia, Common	Phacelia distans	n/c	Boraginaceae	Borage	Hydrophyllaceae	Waterleaf
Phacelia, California	Phacelia egena	n/c	Boraginaceae	Borage	Hydrophyllaceae	Waterleaf
Nemophila, Small-flowered	Nemophila parviflora var. p.	Nemophila parviflora	Boraginaceae	Borage	Hydrophyllaceae	Waterleaf
Eucrypta, Common	Eucrypta chrysanthemifolia	n/c	Boraginaceae	Borage	Hydrophyllaceae	Waterleaf
Phacelia, Stinging	Phacelia malvifolia	n/c	Boraginaceae	Borage	Hydrophyllaceae	Waterleaf
Fiesta Flower	Pholistoma auritum var. a.	n/c	Boraginaceae	Borage	Hydrophyllaceae	Waterleaf
Baby Blue Eyes	Nemophila menziesii var. m.	Nemophila menziesii	Boraginaceae	Borage	Hydrophyllaceae	Waterleaf
Phacelia, Imbricate	Phacelia imbricata ssp. i.	Phacelia imbricata	Boraginaceae	Borage	Hydrophyllaceae	Waterleaf
Soap Plant	Chlorogalum pomeridianum var. p.	Chlorogalum pomeridianum	Agavaceae	Century Plant	Liliaceae	Lily
Star Lily, Fremont's	Toxicoscordion fremontii	Zigadenus fremontii	Melanthiaceae	False Hellebore	Liliaceae	Lily

Common Name	Current Scientific Name	Old Scientific Name	Family (Latin)	Family (English)	Old Family (Latin)	Old Family (English)
Trillium	Trillium chloropetalum	n/c	Melanthiaceae	False Hellebore	Liliaceae	Lily
Solomon, Fat	Maianthemum racemosum	Smilacina racemosa	Ruscaceae	Butcher's broom	Liliaceae	Lily
Solomon, Fat	Maianthemum stellatum	Smilacina stellata	Ruscaceae	Butcher's broom	Liliaceae	Lily
Brodiaea, Dwarf	Brodiaea terrestris ssp. terrestris	Brodiaea terrestris	Themidaceae	Brodiaea	Liliaceae	Lily
Blue Dicks / Wild Hyacinth	Dichelostemma capitatum ssp. c.	Dichelostemma capitatum	Themidaceae	Brodiaea	Liliaceae	Lily
Brodiaea, Golden / Pretty Face	Triteleia ixioides ssp. i.	n/c	Themidaceae	Brodiaea	Liliaceae	Lily
Spring Beauty, Red-stemmed	Claytonia rubra ssp. depressa	n/c	Montiaceae	Miner's Lettuce	Portulacaceae	Purslane
Red Maids	Calandrinia ciliata	n/c	Montiaceae	Miner's Lettuce	Portulacaceae	Purslane
Miner's Lettuce	Claytonia perfoliata ssp. p.	n/c	Montiaceae	Miner's Lettuce	Portulacaceae	Purslane
Scarlet Pimpernel	Anagallis arvensis	n/c	Myrsinaceae	Myrsine	Primulaceae	Primrose
Star Flower	Trientalis latifolia	n/c	Myrsinaceae	Myrsine	Primulaceae	Primrose
Paintbrush, Coast / Indian	Castilleja affinis ssp. a.	Castilleja affinis	Orobanchaceae	Broomrape	Scrophulariaceae	Figwort
Owl's Clover, Narrow-leaved	Castilleja attenuata	n/c	Orobanchaceae	Broomrape	Scrophulariaceae	Figwort
Owl's Clover, Dense Flower	Castilleja densiflora ssp. d.	n/c	Orobanchaceae	Broomrape	Scrophulariaceae	Figwort
Owl's Clover, Pink	Castilleja exserta ssp. e.	n/c	Orobanchaceae	Broomrape	Scrophulariaceae	Figwort
Indian Paintbrush, Woolly	Castilleja foliolosa	n/c	Orobanchaceae	Broomrape	Scrophulariaceae	Figwort
Bird's Beak	Cordylanthus rigidus ssp. r.	n/c	Orobanchaceae	Broomrape	Scrophulariaceae	Figwort
Indian Warrior	Pedicularis densiflora	n/c	Orobanchaceae	Broomrape	Scrophulariaceae	Figwort
Owl's Clover, Dwarf	Triphysaria pusillus	n/c	Orobanchaceae	Broomrape	Scrophulariaceae	Figwort
Monkey Flower, Sticky	Mimulus aurantiacus	n/c	Phrymaceae	Lopseed	Scrophulariaceae	Figwort

Common Name	Current Scientific Name	Old Scientific Name	Family (Latin)	Family (English)	Old Family (Latin)	Old Family (English)
Monkey Flower, Santa Lucia Sticky	Mimulus aurantiacus var. bifidus	n/c	Phrymaceae	Lopseed	Scrophulariaceae	Figwort
Monkeyflower, Seep	Mimulus guttatus	n/c	Phrymaceae	Lopseed	Scrophulariaceae	Figwort
Snapdragon, Kellogg's	Antirrhinum kelloggii	n/c	Plantaginaceae	Plantain	Scrophulariaceae	Figwort
Snapdragon, Sticky	Antirrhinum multiflorum	n/c	Plantaginaceae	Plantain	Scrophulariaceae	Figwort
Chinese Houses	Collinsia heterophylla var. h.	Collinsia heterophylla	Plantaginaceae	Plantain	Scrophulariaceae	Figwort
Toad Flax, Blue	Nuttallanthus texanus	Linaria canadensis	Plantaginaceae	Plantain	Scrophulariaceae	Figwort
Toad-flax, Cloven-lip	Linaria bipartita	n/c	Plantaginaceae	Plantain	Scrophulariaceae	Figwort
Scarlet Bugler	Penstemon centranthifolius	n/c	Plantaginaceae	Plantain	Scrophulariaceae	Figwort
Brooklime, American	Veronica americana	n/c	Plantaginaceae	Plantain	Scrophulariaceae	Figwort
Speedwell, Broad-fruited Water	Veronica catenata	n/c	Plantaginaceae	Plantain	Scrophulariaceae	Figwort
Blue-eyed Mary, Child's	Collinsia childii	n/c	Plantaginaceae	Plantain	Scrophulariaceae	Figwort
Speedwell, Persian	Veronica persica	n/c	Plantaginaceae	Plantain	Scrophulariaceae	Figwort
Fremontia	Fremontodendron californicum	n/c	Malvaceae	Mallow	Sterculiaceae	Cacao

Part 2 - Changes in Genus or Species names

Common Name	Current Scientific Name	Old Scientific Name	Family - Latin	Family - English
Aster, California	Symphyotrichum chilense	Aster chilensis	Asteraceae	Sunflower
Aster, Rough-leaved	Eurybia radulina	Aster radulinus	Asteraceae	Sunflower
Burnet, Small / Salad	Poterium sanguisorba	Sanguisorba minor ssp. muricata	Rosaceae	Rose
Butterweed, Brewer's	Packera beweri	Senecio breweri	Asteraceae	Sunflower

Common Name	Current Scientific Name	Old Scientific Name	Family - Latin	Family - English
Centaury, Davy's	Zeltnera davyi	Centaurium davyi	Gentianaceae	Gentian
Cinquefoil, Sticky	Drymocallis glandulosa var. wrangeliana	Potentilla glandulosa	Rosaceae	Rose
Coffeeberry, California	Frangula californica ssp. c.	Rhamnus californica ssp. occidentalis	Rhamnaceae	Buckthorn
Coffeeberry, Hoary	Frangula californica ssp. tomentella	Rhamnus tomentolla ssp. tomentolla	Rhamnaceae	Buckthorn
Cotton-batting Plant	Pseudognaphalium stramineum	Gnaphalium stramineum	Asteraceae	Sunflower
Cudweed, California	Pseudognaphalium californicum	Gnaphalium californicum	Asteraceae	Sunflower
Cudweed, Purple	Gamochaeta ustulata	Gnaphalium purpureum	Asteraceae	Sunflower
Cudweed, Weedy	Pseudognaphalium luteoalbum	Gnaphalium luteo-album	Asteraceae	Sunflower
Deerweed	Acmispon glaber var. g.	Lotus scoparius	Fabaceae	Pea
Everlasting, Fragrant	Pseudognaphalium beneolens	Gnaphalium canescens ssp. beneolens	Asteraceae	Sunflower
Everlasting, Pink	Pseudognaphalium ramosissimum	Gnaphalium ramosissimum	Asteraceae	Sunflower
Fairy Bells	Prosartes hookeri	Disporum hookeri	Liliaceae	Lily
Fiddleneck	Amsinckia intermedia	Amsinckia menziesii var. intermedia	Boraginaceae	Borage
Fireweed, Cut-leaved	Senecio glomeratus	Erechtites glomerata	Asteraceae	Sunflower
Goldenrod, California	Solidago velutina ssp. californica	Solidago californica	Asteraceae	Sunflower
Horseweed	Erigeron canadensis	Conyza canadensis	Asteraceae	Sunflower
Knotweed, Common	Polygonum aviculare ssp. depressum	Polygonum arenastrum	Polygonaceae	Knotweed
Linanthus, Bicolored	Leptosiphon bicolor	Linanthus bicolor	Polemoniaceae	Phlox
Linanthus, Common	Leptosiphon parviflorus	Linanthus parviflorus	Polemoniaceae	Phlox
Lotus, Bishop's	Acmispon strigosus	Lotus strigosus	Fabaceae	Pea
Lotus, Chile	Acmispon wrangelianus	Lotus wrangelianus	Fabaceae	Pea
Lotus, Large Flowered / Chaparral	Acmispon grandiflorus var. g.	Lotus grandiflorus	Fabaceae	Pea
Lotus, Spanish	Acmispon americanus var. a.	Lotus purshianus	Fabaceae	Pea

Common Name	Current Scientific Name	Old Scientific Name	Family - Latin	Family - English
Madia, Woodland	Anisocarpus madioides	Madia madioides	Asteraceae	Sunflower
Meconella, Narrow leaved	Hesperomecon linearis	Meconella linearis	Papaveraceae	Poppy
Ox-tongue, Bristly	Helminthotheca echioides	Picris echioides	Asteraceae	Sunflower
Parsnip, Cow	Heracleum maximum	Heracleum lanatum	Apiaceae	Carrot
Phlox, Slender	Microsteris gracilis	Phlox gracilis	Polemoniaceae	Phlox
Pineapple Weed	Matricaria discoidea	Chamomilla suaveolens	Asteraceae	Sunflower
Primrose, Small	Camissoniopsis micrantha	Camissonia micrantha	Onagraceae	Evening Primrose
Saxifrage, California	Micranthes californica	Saxifraga californica	Saxifragaceae	Saxifrage
Suncups	Taraxia ovata	Camissonia ovata	Onagraceae	Evening Primrose
Sweet Cicely, Wood	Osmorhiza berteroi	Osmorhiza chilensis	Apiaceae	Carrot
Tarweed, Coast	Deinandra corymbosa	Hemizonia corymbosa ssp. corymbosa	Asteraceae	Sunflower
Tower Mustard	Turritis glabra	Arabis glabra	Brassicaceae	Mustard
Trefoil, Coastal Bird's Foot	Acmispon maritimus var. m.	Lotus salsuginosus	Fabaceae	Pea
Tule, Common	Schoenoplectus acutus var. occidentalis	Scirpus acutus	Cyperaceae	Sedge
Turkey Mullein	Croton setigerus	Eremocarpus setigerus	Euphorbiaceae	Spurge
Watercress	Nasturtium officinale	Rorippa nasturtium-aquaticum	Brassicaceae	Mustard
Wood-sorrel, Dwarf	Oxalis micrantha	Oxalis laxa	Oxalidaceae	Oxalis
Wood-sorrel, Hairy	Oxalis pilosa	Oxalis albicans ssp. pilosa	Oxalidaceae	Oxalis
Woolly Marbles, Round	Psilocarphus chilensis	Psilocarphus tenellus var. globiferus	Asteraceae	Sunflower
Yerba Buena	Clinopodium douglasii	Satureja douglasii	Lamiaceae	Mint

Parts of a typical flower

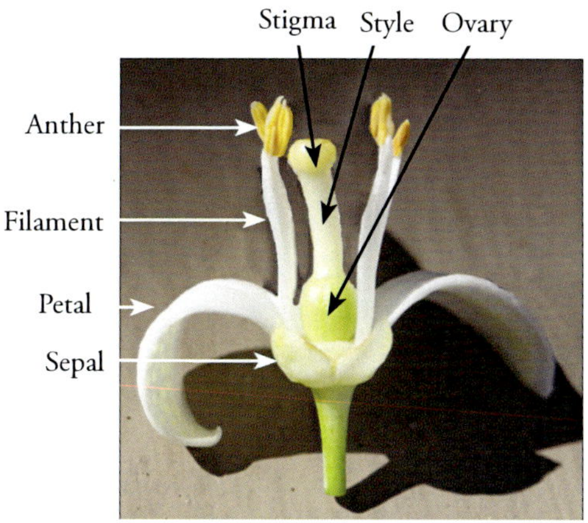

Pistil = Stigma + Style + Ovary
Stamen = Anther + Filament

Substructure of a flower

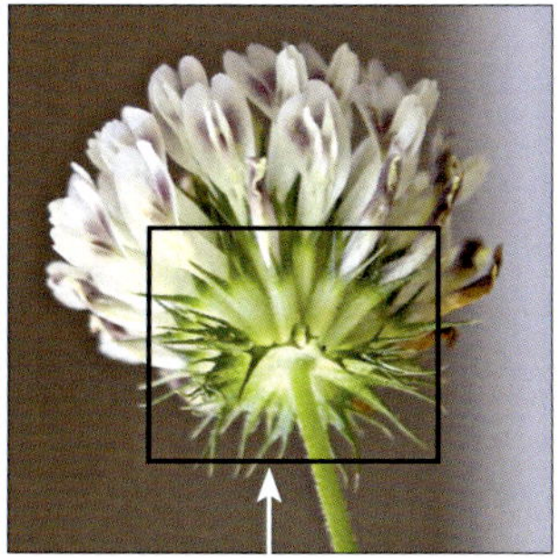

Involucre

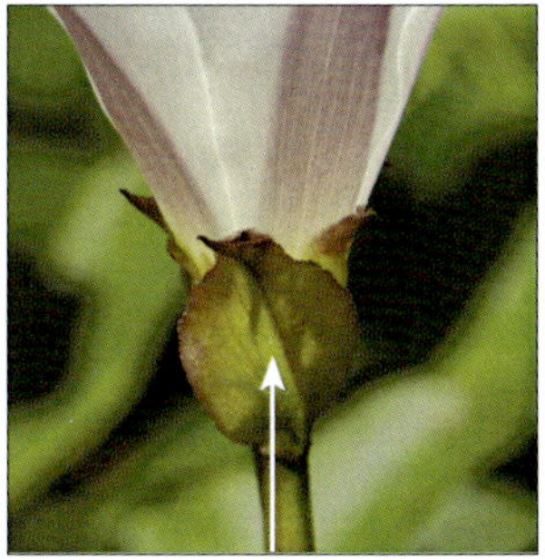

Bract

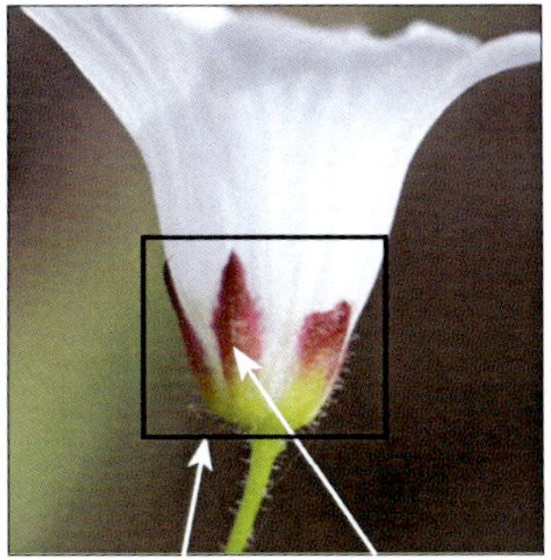

Types of Flowering Heads

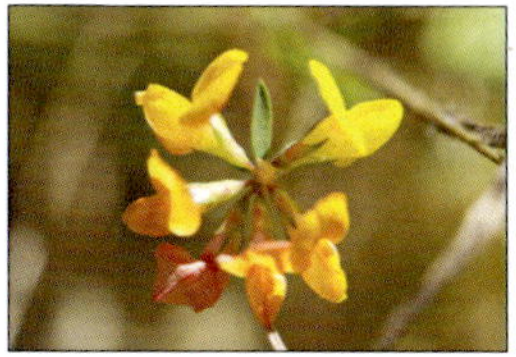

Umbel - simple

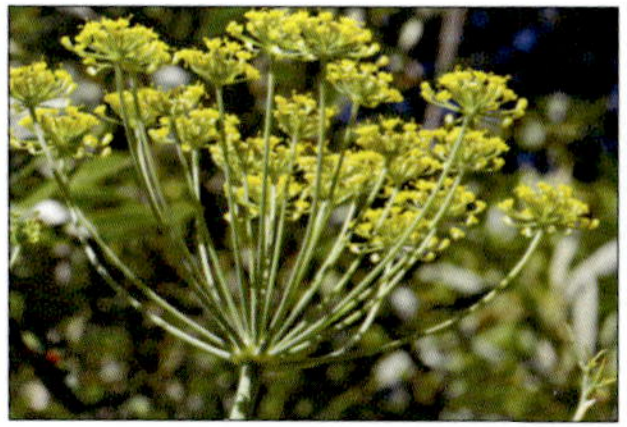

Umbel - compound

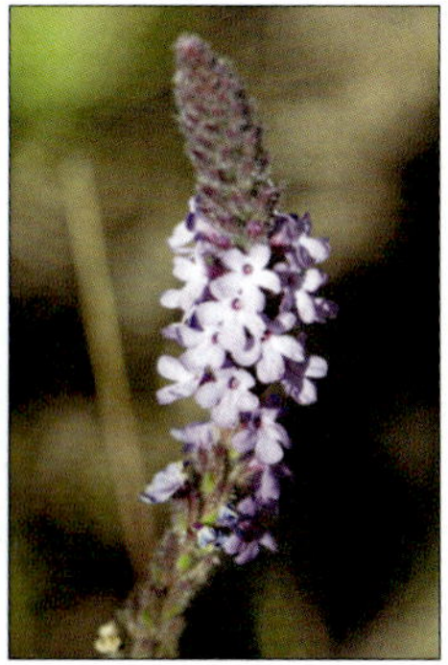

Spike

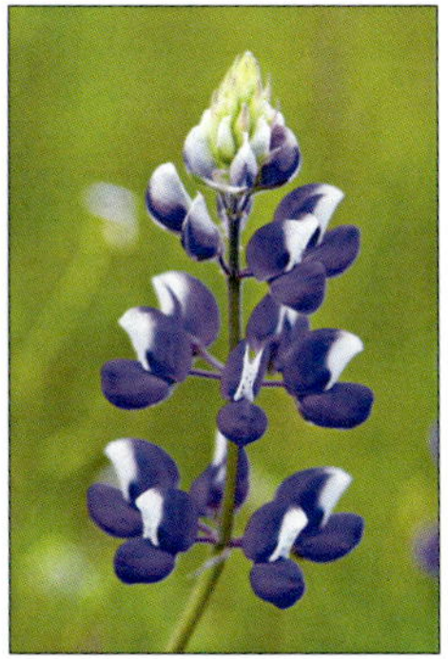

Raceme

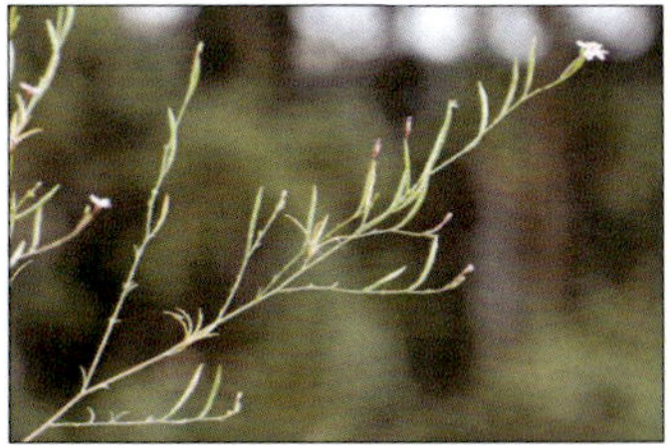

Panicle

Parts of various Asteraceae *(see Glossary and page -v- of Introduction for more details)*

Phyllaries

Ray flower Disk flowers

Ligules

Body Beak Pappus

Fabaceae flower

Banner Keel Wing

Common Leaf Forms

Simple and Serrated

Palmate

Compound & lobed

Simple, lobed & dissected

Clasping

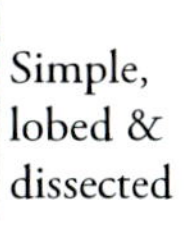

Pinnate

Bipinnate

Fasciculate

Linear to threadlike

Poison Oak
Toxicodendron diversilobum

CAUTION - DO NOT TOUCH

Blooms	Plant Height	Flower size	Origin	Life-form
Apr-May	Variable	Very small	Native	Shrub - Vine-like

'Leaves of three - let it be'

If you only learn one plant at Garland Ranch, this is the one it should be.

All parts of this plant contain an oily resin (urushiol) that can cause a highly unpleasant and irritating rash if touched, even in the dormant winter months. The plant is extremely common and is found in all habitats. It is very variable in appearance, sometimes low growing on or near the trail, sometimes forming large shrubs and sometimes climbing high into trees.

Its leaves resemble those of certain deciduous oaks but usually grow in groups of three. Bright shiny green in spring and early summer, they turn a brilliant red in the fall.

The indigenous people had (or were able to develop) an immunity to poison oak and used it in a variety of ways.

Notes:

Invasive species

Certain non-native species are listed in the California Invasive Plant Inventory published by the California Invasive Plant Council.

Some are highly invasive, some moderately so and others have only a limited impact. A "#" after the region of origin indicates that the species is regarded as invasive.

#	=	limited
##	=	moderate
###	=	high

Life-form abbreviations:

Ann:	Annual
Bienn:	Biennial
Per:	Perennial
S/L per	Short-lived perennial

Changes in Family, Genus or Species:

An asterisk (*) after the Family or Scientific name indicates a change.

Flower / Plant Sizes

The sizing of flowers is an approximate art since flowers can vary widely in size, even on the same plant. The key used in the text is as follows:

Very Small:	<1/4 inch in diameter
Small:	1/4 - 1/2 inch in diameter
Medium:	1/2 to 1 inch in diameter
Large:	>1 inch in diameter

Where flowers appear in clusters (whether racemes or spikes), an approximate size for the cluster is given:

Small Cluster:	<2 inches in height or length
Medium Cluster:	2 - 4 inches in height or length
Large Cluster:	>4 inches in height or length

Periwinkle
Vinca major

Blooms	Plant Height	Flower size	Origin	Life-form
May-July	6-24 in	Medium	Eur ?	Per

A garden escapee, usually found in sun or partially shaded areas, Periwinkle is an aggressive ground cover with dark green glossy foliage and bright bluish-purple flowers. Note the surprisingly slender sepals (lower R).

Forget-me-not
Myosotis latifolia

Blooms	Plant Height	Flower size	Origin	Life-form
Feb-July	4-24 in	Small	NW Africa #	Per

Found both in sunny, sandy places such as trails and also in shaded woodland, these are low growing plants with many small palish blue flowers, similar in shape to certain other members of its family such as the Hound's Tongue, Popcorn Flower and Cryptantha. Grows aggressively in a garden setting if allowed to do so.

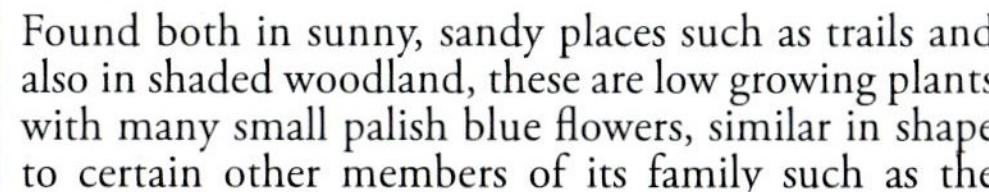

Hound's Tongue
Cynoglossum grande

Blooms	Plant Height	Flower size	Origin	Life-form
Feb-Apr	6-30 in	Small Cluster	Native	Per

One of the first to bloom in the spring, this plant is found in shaded woodland. It has clusters of small blue/purple flowers with an inner row of white teeth growing at the tip of a single stem. Its common name comes from its comparatively large basal leaves which are reminiscent of a panting dog's tongue.

Great Valley Phacelia
Phacelia ciliata

Blooms	Plant Height	Flower size	Origin	Life-form
Mar-May	4-22 in	Small	Native	Ann

Found in open grassland, this plant is generally erect, simple or branched at base, its stem covered with minute soft hairs. The small pale blue flower is funnel to bell-shaped. The exserted stamens are longer than the flower is wide. Note the much enlarged calyx in the numerous fruit with its prominent veins.

Baby Blue-eyes
Nemophila menziesii var. *menziesii*

Blooms	Plant Height	Flower size	Origin	Life-form
Feb-June	4-12 in	Medium	Native	Ann

Found mainly in sunny areas, this flower is quite common in the mid-spring to early summer. Pure white specimens may be found. A less common relative, with a loose, sprawling growth habit, is the tiny (<1 cm) Common Eucrypta (*Eucrypta chrysanthemifolia*) (lower R). Note the blue veins in the petals.

Fiesta Flower
Pholistoma auritum var. *auritum*

Blooms	Plant Height	Flower size	Origin	Life-form
Mar-May	12-40 in	Medium	Native	Ann

Very common in shady areas under oak trees, this plant has a vigorous vine-like growth habit with a profusion of bluish-purple flowers. White flowers are occasionally found. The stems have small hooks which catch and stick to fabric, hence its use as an inexpensive corsage. Note the unusual lobed calyx.

Venus' Looking Glass
Triodanis biflora

Blooms	Plant Height	Flower size	Origin	Life-form
Apr-June	2-16 in	Medium	Native	Ann

Found in sunny areas or partial shade, this produces bell-like pinkish-purple flowers, opening up as they mature. There are comparatively few specimens in Garland Ranch. Note the leaf-like bracts clasping the sessile flower.

Purple Sand Spurry
Spergularia rubra

Blooms	Plant Height	Flower size	Origin	Life-form
Apr-Sept	<2 in	Small	Medit, Asia	Ann - S/L per

Found in sunny, sandy places, this low-growing plant has many small flowers with green to purplish sepals visible between the pink to lavender petals. Note the 3-lobed stigma projecting from the ovary which helps differentiate this plant from the much larger white-flowered Spurry (*Spergula arvensis*).

Tree Lupine / Yellow Bush Lupine
Lupinus arboreus

Blooms	Plant Height	Flower size	Origin	Life-form
Mar-June	<6.5 ft	Large Clusters	Native	Shrub

This bush is found in shady but more usually in open sunny places. It can grow quite large and the sweet-smelling flowers, despite their common name, can be yellow, lilac blue, pink or even white, sometimes in combination. They may or may not be whorled. The Silver Bush Lupine has a similar growth habit but is distinguished by its dark purple flowers and silvery leaves.

Silver Bush Lupine
Lupinus albifrons var. *albifrons*

Blooms	Plant Height	Flower size	Origin	Life-form
Mar-June	<6.5 ft	Large Clusters	Native	Shrub

This bush is found in open sunny places. It can grow quite large with dark purple flowers and distinctive silvery leaves. The flowers tend to be either not or only loosely whorled. The Tree Lupine *(L. arboreus)* is distinguishable by its paler (and more variable in color) flowers and green leaves. Note also the cilia (small hairs) only on the upper part of the keel, the Tree Lupine is ciliate along the length of the keel and the Summer Lupine *(L. formosus)* has no cilia at all.

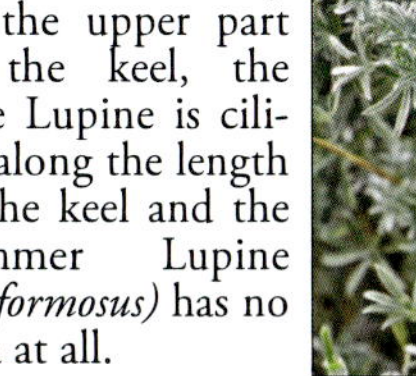

Summer Lupine
Lupinus formosus var. *formosus*

Blooms	Plant Height	Flower size	Origin	Life-form
Apr-Oct	8-30 in	Large Clusters	Native	Per

This lupine is found in open sunny places, sometimes in profusion. The leaves are superficially similar to the Silver Bush Lupine *(L. albifrons),* gray-green and with minute hairs, but the plant is lower growing, the flower paler in color and, most important, the keel has a total absence of cilia whereas the Silver Bush Lupine has noticeable cilia on the upper part of the keel.

Broad-leaved Lupine
Lupinus latifolius var. *latifolius*

Blooms	Plant Height	Flower size	Origin	Life-form
Mar-June	2-5 ft	Large Clusters	Native	Per

A shade loving plant, this is comparatively tall and most easily recognized by its broad leaves. As with all Lupines, the leaflets grow in whorls on the stems. The flowers are sometimes whorled. The flowers can be variable in color but in Garland Ranch are most typically pale to mid-purple. The petals turn brown as they age.

Sky Lupine
Lupinus nanus

Blooms	*Plant Height*	*Flower size*	*Origin*	*Life-form*
May-June	8-20 in	Large Clusters	Native	Ann

This is a very common, fragrant plant. It is found in open sunny places, often in large numbers producing a spectacular display. Individual flowers are blue/purple with a purple dotted narrowish white stripe on the banner which turns reddish or violet after pollination. Note that the banner wraps around more deeply than the Miniature Lupine (*L. bicolor*). The flowers are whorled.

Lindley's Annual Lupine / Miniature Lupine
Lupinus bicolor

Blooms	*Plant Height*	*Flower size*	*Origin*	*Life-form*
May-June	4-16 in	Small Clusters	Native	Ann

This is a low, fairly inconspicuous flower, found in open sunny places. Easily confused with a small Sky Lupine (*L. nanus*), but the white on the banner is broader than on the Sky Lupine and the banner itself is taller than it is wide (the reverse of the Sky Lupine) and wraps around less. The flowers grow in whorls with shorter stems towards the top of the raceme.

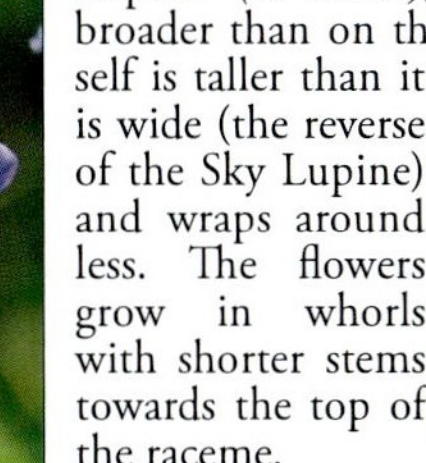

Stinging Lupine
Lupinus hirsutussimus

Blooms	Plant Height	Flower size	Origin	Life-form
Mar-May	8-40 in	Large Clusters	Native	Ann

Found in open sunny or sometimes disturbed places. The flowers are bright pink to magenta and not whorled. The stems have noticeable stiff hairs and the leaves are broad and hairy with a bumpy or blistered appearance.

Nuttall's Annual Lupine
Lupinus truncatus

Blooms	Plant Height	Flower size	Origin	Life-form
Mar-May	8-20 in	Large Clusters	Native	Ann

This lupine is found in open sunny places. The flowers are dark red-purple and with a comparatively small number of individual flowers on each stem. The flowers are not whorled. The leaves are very narrow with squarish ends which gives the species its Latin name.

Alfalfa
Medicago sativa

Blooms	Plant Height	Flower size	Origin	Life-form
Apr-Oct	16-36 in	Med Clusters	Eurasia	Per

This plant can form a medium-sized shrub with a mass of bluish-purple flowers. It is widely used as a forage crop, both in the USA and elsewhere and its sprouts are a popular addition to salads and sandwiches. Worldwide production of Alfalfa exceeds 400m tons per annum.

California Tea
Rupertia physodes

Blooms	Plant Height	Flower size	Origin	Life-form
Apr-June	12-24 in	Med Clusters	Native	Per

This plant forms a smallish low growing shrub, found in both shade and sunny places, often in extended patches. The common name derives from the shape of the leaves which resemble those of the tea plant.

Douglas Iris
Iris douglasiana

Blooms	Plant Height	Flower size	Origin	Life-form
Mar-May	6-30 in	Large	Native	Per-Rhizome

Found on grassy slopes in woodland and in canyons, there are comparatively few specimens of this common but beautiful Iris to be found in Garland Ranch. The inflorescence comprises 3 long petal-like sepals which are broad and down-curving and 3-6 narrower and more erect petals. 'Iris' comes from the Greek word for rainbow.

Blue-eyed Grass
Sisyrinchium bellum

Blooms	Plant Height	Flower size	Origin	Life-form
Mar-May	4-16 in	Medium	Native	Per-Rhizome

Very commonly found by trails and in open grassland, this flower is more purple than blue and with a vivid yellow eye. The 'blue' in the name refers to the color of the petal rather than the eye. A white form is not uncommon.

Chia
Salvia columbariae

Blooms	Plant Height	Flower size	Origin	Life-form
Mar-June	4-20 in	Small	Native	Ann

Found in open sunny areas, Chia produces vivid blue flowers on its reddish-brown heads. Its seeds were (and still are) highly prized for their nutritional value and their ability to retain water. It is said that indigenous people could keep going for an entire day by keeping a small handful of Chia seeds in their mouths.

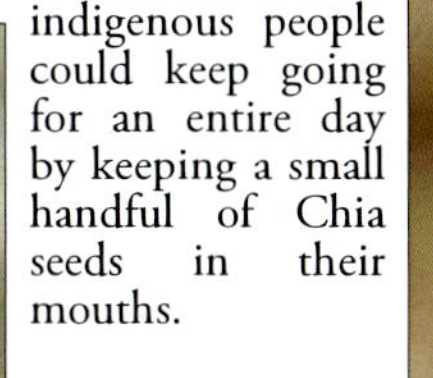

Dannie's Skullcap
Scutellaria tuberosa

Blooms	Plant Height	Flower size	Origin	Life-form
Mar-July	<10 in	Small	Native	Per

A small low growing plant, usually found in early spring in sunny or partially shaded areas along trails. The shape of the upper part of the flower is reminiscent of the skullcaps worn by the French Revolutionaries (which also gave their name to Liberty Cap in Yosemite).

Vinegar Weed
Trichostema lanceolatum

Blooms	Plant Height	Flower size	Origin	Life-form
July-Oct	4-24 in	Medium	Native	Ann

Found in dry sunny areas, this is a fairly small, rather dull plant with small but very distinctive bluish-purple flowers. Note the long, strongly curved, exserted and fused stamens and pistils extending from the U-shaped flower tube The foliage contains a volatile oil which gives off a strong vinegary smell if touched. If hot, it can be smelled before it is seen.

Naked Broomrape
Orobanche uniflora

Blooms	Plant Height	Flower size	Origin	Life-form
Mar-July	<4 in	Small	Native	Ann / Per

This tiny flower, like almost all other members of its family, is parasitic, in this case on members of the Sunflower or Saxifrage families. Its beautiful bluish-purple flowers are unmistakable if one is fortunate enough to spot the flower in the first place. The plant has no leaves and most of the plant is found underground.

Chinese Houses
Collinsia heterophylla

Blooms	Plant Height	Flower size	Origin	Life-form
May-June	2-5 in	Large Clusters	Native	Ann

Chinese Houses are found in both sun and shade; usually in groups and sometimes in very large numbers. Leaves are opposite. The medium to dark purple flowers are arranged in tiered layers of 3-5 blossoms in a row giving a pagoda-like appearance. Heterophylla means the leaves are different on the same plant.

Child's Blue-eyed Mary
Collinsia childii

Blooms	Plant Height	Flower size	Origin	Life-form
May-June	4-16 in	Medium	Native	Ann

This is rarely found in Garland Ranch. A relative of Chinese Houses *(C. heterophylla)*, it is a low growing, slightly sprawling plant with small bluish-purple flowers and lanceolate, opposite leaves. Note the slightly hairy stem and calyx which serve to distinguish this from other Collinsias. The flower heads bear between 2 and 5 blooms.

Kellogg's / Lax Snapdragon
Antirrhinum kelloggii

Blooms	Plant Height	Flower size	Origin	Life-form
Mar-May	2-30 in	Small	Native	Ann - Vine-like

This is a rare find in Garland Ranch. Its beautiful flowers are not unlike the Blue Toad-flax *(Nuttalanthus canadensis)* but it has no spur and its sprawling, vine-like growth habit is quite distinct. It appears to like burnt or disturbed areas though it is found in other areas as well.

Blue Toad-flax
Nuttalanthus texanus *

Blooms	Plant Height	Flower size	Origin	Life-form
Mar-May	4-24 in	Small	Native	Ann / Bienn

Less dramatic than its Moroccan relative, the Cloven-lip Toad-flax *(Linaria bipartita)*, this delicate bluish-purple flower with its 1 inch long pointed spur is usually found in open grassland. The upper lip is slightly lobed and the lower lip is much broader than the upper with a pale ridge in the center.

Cloven-lip Toad-flax
Linaria bipartita

Blooms	Plant Height	Flower size	Origin	Life-form
Feb-June	4-12 in	Med Cluster	Medit	Ann

A garden escapee, native to Morocco, this has tall very thin leaves and brightly colored flower heads, sometimes bluish-purple with yellow and white, sometimes red and sometimes creamy-yellow. Like the Blue Toad Flax, the flowers each have a long narrow spur. The lower lip is prominently inflated, hence the common name.

American Brooklime
Veronica americana

Blooms	Plant Height	Flower size	Origin	Life-form
May-Aug	2-24 in	Small	Native	Ann

Closely related to Persian Speedwell *(V. persica)*, this prefers very wet conditions, in or by stream beds. The petals have specks of red in them and dark veins radiating from the center. The opposite leaves are larger and more pointed than those of the Persian Speedwell.

Persian Speedwell / Bird's Eye Speedwell
Veronica persica

Blooms	Plant Height	Flower size	Origin	Life-form
Feb-May	4-16 in	Small	Asia Minor	Ann

Found in shade, sometimes on the trail, this low growing and inconspicuous plant produces a number of small bright blue and white flowers. It not uncommonly appears as a weed in lawns. The flower is very similar to American Brooklime *(V. americana)* but prefers a dryer habitat.

Broad-Fruited & Great Water Speedwell
Veronica catenata & Veronica anagallis-aquatica

Blooms	Plant Height	Flower size	Origin	Life-form
July-Sept	4-24 in	Small	Eur	Per

Usually found by water, these Speedwells have paler flowers than the American Brooklime or Persian Speedwell. The two are very similar but can be distinguished by the much smaller flowers and longer, narrower leaves of the Broad Fruited Water Speedwell and by the distinct notch in its fruits. The Great Water Speedwell's fruits have either no or a barely discernible notch.

Statice
Limonium sinuatum

Blooms	Plant Height	Flower size	Origin	Life-form
June-Oct	12-20 in	Med Clusters	Medit / W. Asia	Ann

An introduced species, this plant is found in dry sunny areas and is unmistakable with its papery purple or sometimes pale lavender or white sepals and white petalled-flowers. It is sometimes known as Wavyleaf Sea Lavender, though unrelated to true lavenders.

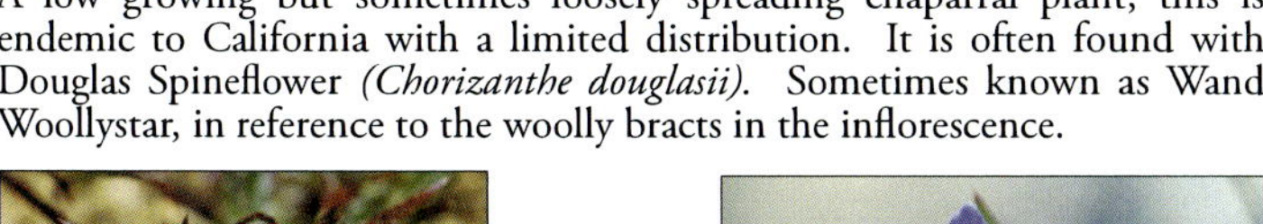

Virgate Eriastrum
Eriastrum virgatum

Blooms	Plant Height	Flower size	Origin	Life-form
May-July	4-8 in	Small	Native	Ann

A low growing but sometimes loosely spreading chaparral plant, this is endemic to California with a limited distribution. It is often found with Douglas Spineflower *(Chorizanthe douglasii)*. Sometimes known as Wand Woollystar, in reference to the woolly bracts in the inflorescence.

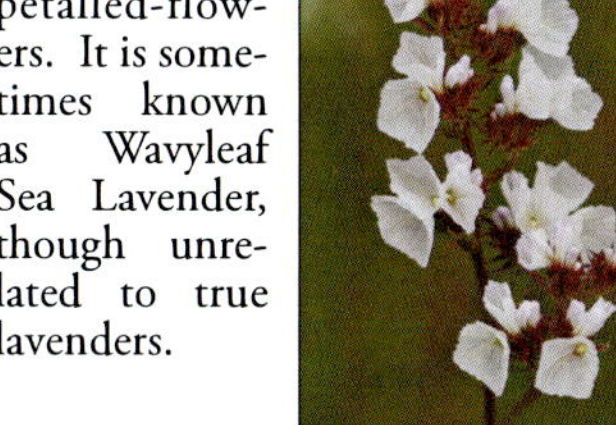

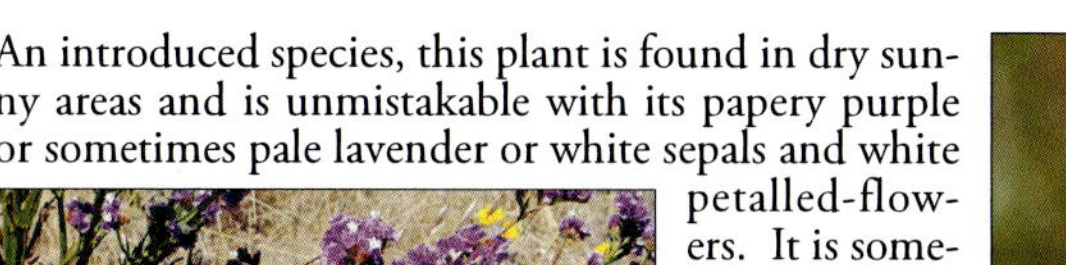

California Gilia
Gilia achilleifolia ssp. *achilleifolia*

Blooms	Plant Height	Flower size	Origin	Life-form
May-June	2-28 in	Small Clusters	Native	Ann

Unlike most of the other Gilias to be found in Garland Ranch, this produces 8-25 pale blue flowers (with 5 petals) in clusters. A favorite of butterflies such as the Chalcedon Checkerspot (lower L). Note the thin, feathery leaves on the stem, similar to those on the Many-stemmed Gilia but a marked contrast with the leafless stems of Blue Dicks.

Many-stemmed Gilia
Gilia achilleifolia ssp. *multicaulis*

Blooms	Plant Height	Flower size	Origin	Life-form
May-June	2-28 in	Small Clusters	Native	Ann

Easily confused with the California Gilia (*G. a.* ssp. *achilleifolia*) and often found growing with it, the flowers of this sub-species are very similar but the plant can be distinguished most easily by the smaller number of flowers in the inflorescence; there being only 1-7 flowers in the flower head as against the 8-25 for the California Gilia.

Holly-leaved Navarretia
Navarretia atractyloides

Blooms	Plant Height	Flower size	Origin	Life-form
May-June	2-12 in	Small	Native	Ann

This is an inconspicuous but common plant to be found on or next to the trails in open sunny areas. It is very similar to the Hooked Navarretia *(N. hamata)* but lacks the skunky smell and the tip of its bracts are not as sharply down curved, instead more or less following the line of the leaf.

Hooked Navarretia
Navarretia hamata

Blooms	Plant Height	Flower size	Origin	Life-form
May-June	3-12 in	Small	Native	Ann

Less common than the Holly-leaved Navarretia, *(N. atractyloides)* this plant also is found on or next to the trails in open sunny areas. It is very similar to the Holly-leaved Navarretia but can be distinguished by its skunky smell and the fact that the tip of its bracts are sharply (almost 90°) down curved.

Honey-scented Navarretia
Navarretia mellita

Blooms	Plant Height	Flower size	Origin	Life-form
May-June	4-8 in	Small	Native	Ann

Similar in appearance to Skunkweed *(N. squarrosa),* but noticeably smaller; this has a sweet smell in sharp contrast to the skunky aroma given off by its eponymous relative. The flowers are light blue to lavender. There are single soft spines at the tip of its bracts and red stems which help differentiate it from Skunkweed.

Skunkweed
Navarretia squarrosa

Blooms	Plant Height	Flower size	Origin	Life-form
June-Aug	4-24 in	Small	Native	Ann

Found in open sunny areas, Skunkweed has a softer, more compact head than the Holly Leaf or Hooked Navarretias and is distinctly oily with an unmistakably skunky smell. The stems are greenish to purplish and the flowers are bluer than the Honey-scented Navarretia.

Coast Larkspur / Zigzag Larkspur
Delphinium patens ssp. *patens*

Blooms	Plant Height	Flower size	Origin	Life-form
Mar-May	4-35 in	Medium	Native	Per

This is a spectacular dark blue to purple flower found in both shade and sun. The long spur is one of the 5 large sepals. In this species the spur is straight or pointing upward. The lower petals in the center of the flower have central hairs and are strongly bi-lobed. Note the comparatively broad leaves with 3-5 divisions.

Parry's Larkspur
Delphinium parryi ssp. *parryi*

Blooms	Plant Height	Flower size	Origin	Life-form
April-May	4-42 in	Medium	Native	Per

Flowering slightly later than the Coast Larkspur (*D. patens*), the flowers are similar but the Parry's Larkspur can be distinguished by its very narrow almost threadlike leaves, though these die back before the flowering season finishes. The spur may be almost an inch long and is usually straight.

Dwarf Ceanothus
Ceanothus dentatus

Blooms	Plant Height	Flower size	Origin	Life-form
Mar-May	<5 ft	Small Clusters	Native	Shrub

The flowers of this small Ceanothus tend to be deep blue. The shrub is densely branched. The leaves are less than 1/2 inch long and have one main vein and small rounded protuberances on their margins. They are often but not always truncated at the tip.

Warty-leaved Ceanothus
Ceanothus papillosus

Blooms	Plant Height	Flower size	Origin	Life-form
Feb-June	<4.5 ft	Small Clusters	Native	Shrub

This Ceanothus is similar to the Dwarf Ceanothus, with clusters of dark blue flowers. Its leaves are larger, from 1/2 inch to 2 inches long, with one main vein and the edges rolled under. They have many small protuberances, both on the margins and in the body of the leaf. The "papillae" may have a glandular appearance.

Blue Blossom
Ceanothus thyrsiflorus var. *thyrsiflorus*

Blooms	*Plant Height*	*Flower size*	*Origin*	*Life-form*
Mar-June	<20 ft	Med Clusters	Native	Shrub

This large shrub is the most common of the Ceanothus in Garland Ranch. It has dense clusters of tiny complex and fragrant blue flowers. Its smooth 3-veined leaves, which are up to 2 inches long serve to distinguish Blue Blossom from the Dwarf or Warty Leaved Ceanothus.

Blue Witch
Solanum umbelliferum

Blooms	*Plant Height*	*Flower size*	*Origin*	*Life-form*
Jan-Sept	<39 in	Medium	Native	Per - Subshrub

A more striking relative of Douglas' Nightshade, this produces bluish-purple flowers with thick yellow anthers surrounding the style and two small green-centered white dots at the base of each petal. Note the soft hairy leaves which are grayish green as are the stems. It produces small green berries which turn purple in the fall.

Blue Dicks
Dichelostemma capitatum ssp. *capitatum*

Blooms	Plant Height	Flower size	Origin	Life-form
Mar-May	12-30 in	Small Cluster	Native	Per (Corm)

Very common in mid to late spring, this flower grows on moderate to long stems either singly or in groups with small purple clusters of 4-10 flowers. Note the 6 petal-like lobes. Closely related to the Brodiaea genus and now in the same small family. Note the absence of leaves on the stem, (unlike the California Gilia (*G. achilleifolia*).

Dwarf Brodiaea
Brodiaea terrestris ssp. *terrestris*

Blooms	Plant Height	Flower size	Origin	Life-form
Apr-July	<4 in	Medium	Native	Per (Corm)

Found in grassy areas, this is very low growing with inconspicuous foliage and easy to miss. The purple-blue 6-petalled trumpet-shaped flowers appear in clumps of 2-10 flowers.

Western Vervain
Verbena lasiostachys var. *lasiostachys*

Blooms	Plant Height	Flower size	Origin	Life-form
May-Sept	12-30 in	Large Clusters	Native	Per

Commonly found, usually in sunny areas, this plant produces multiple spikes (2-8 in long) of small pale purple flowers. The spikes are about 10 inches long and often decumbent. The toothed, oval, slightly hairy leaves are frequently rough and opposite on hairy square stems.

Robust Vervain
Verbena lasiostachys var. *scabrida*

Blooms	Plant Height	Flower size	Origin	Life-form
May-Sept	12-30 in	Large Clusters	Native	Per

This is a variation of the more commonly found Western Vervain (*V. lasiostachys*) and not always easy to distinguish from it. It can be identified by its brighter green leaves and shorter flower spikes (1.5-4 in long) which are less likely to be decumbent.

Purple Sanicle / Snakeroot
Sanicula bipinnatifida

Blooms	Plant Height	Flower size	Origin	Life-form
Mar-May	5-24 in	Medium	Native	Per

Found in open grassy areas, the Purple Sanicle's flowers are more reddish than purple. At first glance, it may be mistaken for a clover, but its exserted stamens are distinctive as are the leaves. Like all sanicles the flower heads are in loose umbels. The Latin name refers to the leaves and means pinnately cleft (i.e. split part of the way but not forming separate leaflets).

Italian Thistle
Carduus pycnocephalus ssp. *pycnocephalus*

Blooms	Plant Height	Flower size	Origin	Life-form
Apr-June	1-7 ft	Medium	Medit ###	Ann

This thistle is highly invasive and common, especially in dry places. The flowers are in groups of 1-5, typically 3. The flower heads are much smaller than with other thistles. The Slender-flowered Thistle *(C. tenuiflorus)* (lower R) is similar but with paler flowers in groups of 5-20.

Indian Thistle
Cirsium brevistylum

Blooms	Plant Height	Flower size	Origin	Life-form
Apr-Sept	1-12 ft	Large	Native	Ann - S/L per

Usually found in shaded or partly-shaded areas, the most characteristic feature of this thistle is the way in which the leaves subtend and sometimes surround the flower head. This readily distinguishes it from the Cobweb and related Thistles *(C. occidentale)*. The Indian Thistle can reach an impressive height and bear a multitude of flowers.

Bull Thistle
Cirsium vulgare

Blooms	Plant Height	Flower size	Origin	Life-form
June-Oct	1-7 ft	Large	Eur ##	Bienn

A late blooming thistle, with a large round to vase-shaped head and purple crown, this alien and invasive species is to be found in sunny and partly shaded areas. Its leaves are large with long sharp spines at their tips and extend up the stem to just below the flower head. An unfriendly species.

Cobweb Thistle
Cirsium occidentale var. *occidentale*

Blooms	*Plant Height*	*Flower size*	*Origin*	*Life-form*
Apr-July	1-10 ft	Large	Native	Bienn

A common thistle in late spring and early summer, the round heads (red to purple or even white) are covered with spiny phyllaries and are covered in dense cobwebby hairs. Easily confused with the Venus Thistle (*C. o.* var. *venustum*), its phyllaries mostly extend straight out or curve upwards.

Venus Thistle
Cirsium occidentale var. *venustum*

Blooms	*Plant Height*	*Flower size*	*Origin*	*Life-form*
Apr-Aug	2v-10 ft	Large	Native	Bienn

Not as common as the Cobweb Thistle (*C. occidentale*), it tends to be redder in color (though can also be purple or white) and its lower phyllaries tend to be sharply downcurved. The cobwebby hairs are not always as evident as in the Cobweb Thistle. In both, the flower heads are elevated well above the lower leaves.

Bigelow Thistle
Cirsium occidentale var. *californicum*

Blooms	Plant Height	Flower size	Origin	Life-form
Apr-July	2-7 ft	Large	Native	Bienn

Rather less common than the Cobweb or Venus Thistles, the flowers of this thistle are pale pink, lavender or white and its heads are more loosely clustered on longer stems. Its phyllaries are often covered in cobwebby hairs and tend to stick straight out or be upward curving like the Cobweb Thistle. The stems are totally naked 6 inches or more below the flower head.

Milk Thistle
Silybum marianum

Blooms	Plant Height	Flower size	Origin	Life-form
Apr-Aug	1-8 ft	Large	Medit #	Ann-bienn

Common and invasive, especially in dry, open places, this thistle is variable in size from fairly small to large with large purple flowers. The white veined leaves are distinctive, as are the star-like phyllaries with their long, sharp spines projecting out from immediately below the flowers.

California Beach-aster
Corethrogyne filaginifolia

Blooms	Plant Height	Flower size	Origin	Life-form
May-Dec	6-24 in	Medium	Native	Per / Subshrub

Despite its common name, this is found in many communities, including chaparral, frequently on as well as beside the trails. Its leaves and stems are typically grayish and hairy; the leaves rather sparse on the flower stems. The flowers appear either singly or as a group, each at the tip of its own stem.

California Aster
Symphyotrichum chilense *

Blooms	Plant Height	Flower size	Origin	Life-form
June-Dec	16-39 in	Medium	Native	Per

Found in open sunny areas, this is a late bloomer with pale purple, long lasting flowers. The flowers are similar to the California Beach Aster (*Corethrogyne filaginifolia*) but the ray flowers are comparatively longer and more slender. The main difference is the color of the foliage, green for the California Aster.

Leafy Daisy
Erigeron foliosus var. *foliosus*

Blooms	*Plant Height*	*Flower size*	*Origin*	*Life-form*
May-Aug	8-40 in	Medium	Native	Per

Native to Western North America, this plant is a member of the genus sometimes known as fleabane. Found in open sunny positions. The leaves (which may be thin and threadlike or wide and flat) are spread evenly up the stem. It has from 15 to 49 ray flowers as well as a centre of bright yellow disk flowers.

Santa Barbara Wirelettuce
Stephanomeria elata

Blooms	*Plant Height*	*Flower size*	*Origin*	*Life-form*
June-Oct	20-48 in	Medium	Native	Ann

One of three Stephanomerias to be found in Garland Ranch, this likes open sunny positions at higher elevations. It has 8-16 ray flowers, sometimes overlapping. Note the grooved, roughened fruit.

Small Stephanomeria
Stephanomeria exigua ssp. *carotifera*

Blooms	Plant Height	Flower size	Origin	Life-form
June-Oct	8-24 in	Medium	Native	Ann

This has flowers similar to the Tall Stephanomeria, but with only 5 or 6 ray flowers. The flowers grow on distinct peduncles (stems) (unlike the Tall Stephanomeria) and the fruit is grooved but not roughened. Like all of the Stephanomerias, this has milky sap.

Tall Stephanomeria
Stephanomeria virgata ssp. *virgata*

Blooms	Plant Height	Flower size	Origin	Life-form
June-Oct	20-120 in	Medium	Native	Ann

The most common of the Stephanomerias found in Garland Ranch, the flowers of this widely branching plant have fewer ray flowers (5-9) than the Santa Barbara Wirelettuce (*S. elata*) and the flowers (white to pink) are 'sessile', i.e. arising more or less directly from the stems. The fruit is not grooved. The plant has milky sap and prefers a bone dry habitat.

Wild Radish
Raphanus sativus

Blooms	Plant Height	Flower size	Origin	Life-form
Feb-July	16-48 in	Medium	Eur-Medit #	Ann-bienn

A very common plant found in both sun and shade, this has the cruciform flowers characteristic of the mustard family but, unlike many of the mustards with their yellow flowers, Radish flowers appear in a wide range of colors, from pure white to dark pink. It has large coarse leaves. Its fruit is edible and has a mild radish taste.

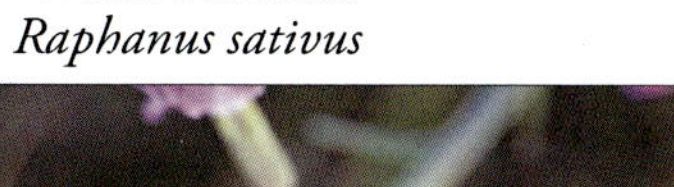

Hairy Honeysuckle
Lonicera hispidula

Blooms	Plant Height	Flower size	Origin	Life-form
Apr-July	6-20 ft	Small Clusters	Native	Shrub

A common shrub, often found climbing in or among trees or other shrubs. Its distinctive pink flowers go on to produce bright red berries. Called 'hairy' because of very small hairs on the flowers themselves. The leaves may be either hairy or smooth. The Chaparral Honeysuckle (*L. interrupta*) is similar, but is hairless (or almost so) and has yellow rather than pink flowers.

Common Snowberry
Symphoricarpos albus var. *laevigatus*

Blooms	Plant Height	Flower size	Origin	Life-form
May-July	2-6 ft	Small Clusters	Native	Shrub

A common straggly shrub, this produces small inconspicuous pink flowers in early summer followed by small berries which turn pure white and remain on the bush through much of the fol-lowing winter. The inside of the berries resembles snow so providing extra justi-fication for the com-mon name.

Creeping Snowberry
Symphoricarpos mollis

Blooms	Plant Height	Flower size	Origin	Life-form
Apr-July	6-24 in	Small Clusters	Native	Shrub

This is very similar to the Common Snowberry (*S. albus* var. *laevigatus*) ex-cept for its height which does not exceed 2 feet. The fruit appears in the mid-late summer as small pure white berries. The berries, like those of the Common Snowberry, are eaten by game birds but are poisonous to humans.

Cretan Rock-rose
Cistus incanus *

Blooms	Plant Height	Flower size	Origin	Life-form
Apr-May	>4 ft	Large	S. Eur	Shrub

Native to the Mediterranean, members of the Rock-rose family all like dry, sunny areas. The shrubs produce a profusion of beautiful short-lived flowers with large wrinkled pink petals. Various species are commonly found in gardens.

Spanish Clover / Spanish Lotus
Acmispon americanus var. *americanus* *

Blooms	Plant Height	Flower size	Origin	Life-form
May-Oct	2-24 in	Small	Native	Ann

This is a common summer plant found in open grassy areas, often in extended patches. It produces a large number of very delicate tiny cream-white to pale pink to red flowers, a little dull at first glance but very beautiful when looked at closely. Long pale gray hairs usually cover this plant.

Leather Root
Hoita macrostachya

Blooms	Plant Height	Flower size	Origin	Life-form
May-Aug	> 6ft	Med Clusters	Native	Per

Found along river or stream banks, this Hoita is a tall, loose-growing plant with lanceolate leaves and long stems bearing clusters of bluish-purple flowers, generally slimmer and longer than those of the Round-leaved Hoita. At Garland Ranch, it blooms a little later than the Round-leaved Hoita.

Round-leaved Hoita
Hoita orbicularis

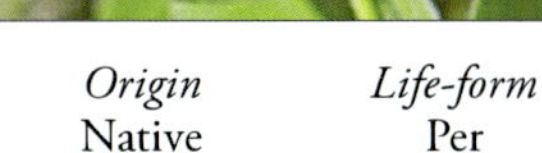

Blooms	Plant Height	Flower size	Origin	Life-form
May-Sept	8-27 in	Med Clusters	Native	Per

This Hoita usually appears in mid-summer alongside creeksides, with profuse leaves and a limited number of reddish-purple pea-shaped flower in clusters. This plant has a creeping stem from which its large, long-stemmed leaves grow. The leaves are divided into 3 rounded leaflets that give off a strong scent. Found only along Garzas Creek along the Redwood Canyon Trail.

Narrow-leaved Clover
Trifolium angustifolium

Blooms	*Plant Height*	*Flower size*	*Origin*	*Life-form*
May-June	4-16 in	Large	Medit	Ann

This is an increasingly common clover, found in open grassy areas, sometimes in large numbers. It is easily distinguished by its cylindrical spike of pink flowers and thin strappy leaves which are almost 2 inches long. There is no involucre. The fruit is surprisingly hard, almost prickly, to the touch.

Bearded Clover
Trifolium barbigerum

Blooms	*Plant Height*	*Flower size*	*Origin*	*Life-form*
April-June	4-12 in	Medium	Native	Ann

This hairy clover has red to purple flowers (usually but not always with a pale tip) and the calyx lobes are plumose. The flowers are held in a bowl-shaped involucre of lobes with toothed edges. The flower head has a long stem.

Rancheria Clover / Indian Clover
Trifolium albopurpureum

Blooms	Plant Height	Flower size	Origin	Life-form
Mar-May	4-16 in	Medium	Native	Ann

Found in open grassy areas in late spring, this clover carpets an area with smallish purple tipped pink and very woolly flowers. The heads are cylindrical and have long flower stems. There are no involucres. Not to be confused with Rose Clover *(T. hirtum)* with its pure pink or white flowers.

Dwarf Sack Clover / Red Sack Clover
Trifolium depauperatum var. *truncatum*

Blooms	Plant Height	Flower size	Origin	Life-form
Apr-June	<6 in	Small	Native	Ann

This clover is found along trails, mainly in sunny areas. It has a very small flower head compared with the more common clovers. The flowers are pink purple with white tips. Involucre lobes are narrowly oblong. The flower head before opening is said to resemble the sack of a cow, hence its common name.

Tree Clover / Foothill Clover
Trifolium ciliolatum

Blooms	*Plant Height*	*Flower size*	*Origin*	*Life-form*
Apr-June	8-20 in	Medium	Native	Ann

This has similar flowers to the Pinpoint Clover *(T. gracilentum)* and can sometimes show the same "pinpoint" but is distinguishable by its longer, more slender leaves and the hairy or bristly calyx on each of the flowers. Note how the each of the flowers become reflexed (hanging down) as the inflorescence matures. There is no involucre.

Rose Clover
Trifolium hirtum

Blooms	*Plant Height*	*Flower size*	*Origin*	*Life-form*
Apr-May	4-16 in	Medium	Eurasia #	Ann

This is a very common, invasive variety carpeting widespread areas with its slightly hairy, beautiful pink flowers. The base of the flower typically has a bract with several small leaves attached. The involucre is replaced by a striped stipule immediately below the flower head and also at the origin of the leaf stem.

Maiden Clover & White Clover
Trifolium microcephalum & Trifolium repens

Blooms	Plant Height	Flower size	Origin	Life-form
Apr-Aug	8-16 in	Medium	Native	Ann

The heads of this clover (also known as Small-headed Clover) are very small with pale pink flowers. Note the prominent bowl-shaped involucre. Found on streambanks and other moist, disturbed areas.

The White Clover (lower R) is a common species, not native and an escapee from cultivation. It also likes damp conditions. It has no involucre.

Creek Clover
Trifolium obtusiflorum

Blooms	Plant Height	Flower size	Origin	Life-form
Apr-July	6-16 in	Medium	Native	Ann

A comparatively unusual clover, most often found in or by stream beds, this is distinguished by its whitish-pink flowers with purple blotches in the center and its sharply serrated leaves. The involucre is deeply cut. The plant is sticky with short glandular hairs.

Tomcat Clover
Trifolium willdenovii

Blooms	Plant Height	Flower size	Origin	Life-form
Mar-June	6-12 in	Medium	Native	Ann

This is very commonly found along trails, in both sun and shade. Note the narrow lanceolate leaves. It has a wheel-like involucre with sharp points which is visible below the flowers in the upper photograph. The flowers are purple with white tips. The Pinpoint Clover is similar but, even when the pinpoint is not visible, can be distinguished by its rounder leaves and the absence of an involucre.

Pinpoint Clover
Trifolium gracilentum

Blooms	Plant Height	Flower size	Origin	Life-form
Apr-June	6-12 in	Medium	Native	Ann

This is found along trails, in both sun and shade. Note the oval leaves (compared to the lanceolate leaves of the Tomcat Clover (*T. willdenovii*)). Note also how each of the flowers become reflexed (hanging down) as the inflorescence matures revealing the pinpoint extending from the tip of the stem. There is no involucre.

Subterranean Clover
Trifolium subterraneum

Blooms	Plant Height	Flower size	Origin	Life-form
Mar-May	4-16 in	Small	S Eur	Ann

A low growing and retiring clover with small whitish-pink flowers with maroon veins; this looks more like a Lotus than a Clover and could be mistaken for the Spanish Clover *(Acmispon americanus)*. The plant is lower and the flowering season much earlier. Note also the longer and slimmer banner.

Cow Clover
Trifolium wormskioldii

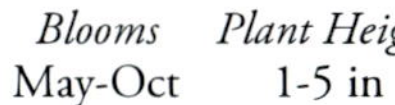

Blooms	Plant Height	Flower size	Origin	Life-form
May-Oct	1-5 in	Medium	Native	Per

A low growing clover with a comparatively large flower, this is more common by the coast, where it can be found in great numbers, usually in wet areas. Its pale pink flowers are quite distinctive. It has a wheel shaped involucre. The leaves (which can be up to 2 in long) are slightly serrated with bristly teeth.

Common Pacific Pea
Lathyrus vestitus var. *vestitus*

Blooms	*Plant Height*	*Flower size*	*Origin*	*Life-form*
Mar-May	[sprawling]	Medium	Native	Per

This is a common vine-like plant with clusters of pinkish-purple and white flowers surrounding the stem and long leaf stems with oval opposite leaves. It is distinguishable from Winter Vetch *(Vicia villosa)* by its lighter coloring and from the Spring Vetch *(Vicia sativa)* by the larger number of individual flowers in each cluster. Older flowers turn brown with age and remain on the stem.

Spring Vetch & Narrow-leaved Vetch
Vicia sativa ssp. *sativa* & ssp. *nigra*

Blooms	*Plant Height*	*Flower size*	*Origin*	*Life-form*
Apr-June	[Vine]	Medium	Eur	Ann

A common species, usually found in open grassland, this has a sprawling growth habit. Its flowers, pink with red (ssp. *sativa,* above) or a more uniform pale purple (ssp. *nigra,* below), appear singly or in pairs. It has 4-8 pairs of opposite leaflets whose blunt tips have tiny bristles. The leaflets of ssp. *nigra* (below) are longer and narrower than those of ssp. *sativa* (above).

Giant Vetch
Vicia gigantea

Blooms	*Plant Height*	*Flower size*	*Origin*	*Life-form*
May-June	12-40 in	Med Clusters	Native	Per

The flowers of this vetch (which, like the Winter Vetch (*V. villosa*), grow on one side of its stems) are reddish-purple turning black with age and forming pendulous clusters of large pods. The leaf stems contain 16-24 leaflets which, unlike those of the Winter Vetch, are progressively smaller towards the end of the stem.

Winter Vetch / Smooth Vetch
Vicia villosa ssp. *varia*

Blooms	*Plant Height*	*Flower size*	*Origin*	*Life-form*
Apr-July	12-48 in	Large Clusters	Eur	Ann

This is a common plant, found in both shade and open grassland, sometimes in great profusion It bears its many flowers in long clusters on one side of its long stems. There are 8-12 pairs of equal-sized linear leaflets per leaf. The common name may be explained by the plant's use as winter forage. Unlike the Woolly Vetch (*V.v.* ssp. *villosa*), it has few hairs on its leaves and stems.

Davy's Centaury
Zeltnera davyi *

Blooms	Plant Height	Flower size	Origin	Life-form
May-Aug	1-10 in	Small	Native	Ann

This is a delightful small flower, normally appearing for a fairly short time in early summer. It is found in open sunny positions, usually in small groups but sometimes in great numbers. The normal color is bright pink with a white center, but a pure creamy-white variant is also common.

Long-beaked Filaree
Erodium botrys

Blooms	Plant Height	Flower size	Origin	Life-form
Mar-July	4-36 in	Medium	Eur	Ann

This is a very common plant found in open grassland and disturbed areas. Note the wine-colored veins on the petals, the red stripe on the calyx, and the cup-shaped flowers. Its most distinctive feature is its very long seed heads (twice as long as those of the Red-stemmed Filaree) which give the plant its common names. Also known as Big Heron's Bill. Leaves are simple.

Red-stemmed Filaree
Erodium cicutarium

Blooms	Plant Height	Flower size	Origin	Life-form
Feb-May	4-20 in	Small	Eurasia ##	Ann

This invasive species is very commonly found on trails and in open grassy areas. Like the other Filarees, it produces longish seed heads which end in a tightly wound spiral. Leaves are pinnate and the leaflets deeply lobed or divided. The stems are slender and usually red.

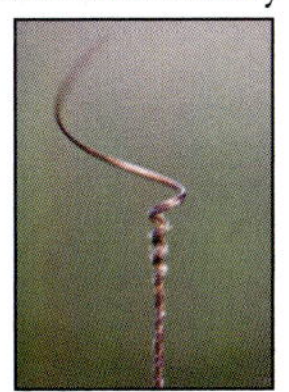

White-stemmed Filaree
Erodium moschatum

Blooms	Plant Height	Flower size	Origin	Life-form
Feb-May	4-24 in	Small	Eur	Ann

Less common than the Red-stemmed Filaree *(E. cicutarium)* but with similar flowers, this can be distinguished by its fat, whitish stem, its simple leaves, less deeply cut, and its tendency to produce multiple flowers and seed heads. The coiled seed heads get caught in other vegetation and unwind and germinate when the next rains come.

Cut-leaved Geranium
Geranium dissectum

Blooms	Plant Height	Flower size	Origin	Life-form
Mar-May	8-30 in	Small	Eur/N Afr/W Asia	Ann

A common, moderately invasive species, this is distinguished by its intense color and the deeply divided segments of its leaves. Note the sharp bristle at the tip of the sepals. Like the Filarees, the Geraniums have beaked fruit but the beak is generally shorter than the Filarees.

Dove's Foot Geranium
Geranium molle

Blooms	Plant Height	Flower size	Origin	Life-form
Jan-June	4-16 in	Small	Eur/N Afr/W Asia	Ann

The most common of the Geraniums in Garland Ranch, the leaves are similar to those sometimes found on the Round-leaved Geranium *(G. rotundifolium)* although more rounded, deeply dissected and palmately-shaped. Its deeply cleft petals are very distinctive, appearing as five sets of twin petals. Sometimes found in a pure white form.

Robert Geranium / Herb Robert
Geranium robertianum

Blooms	*Plant Height*	*Flower size*	*Origin*	*Life-form*
Apr-June	4-28 in	Small	Eur	Ann-bienn

Widespread, though not common in Garland Ranch, this geranium has more rounded petals than the other subspecies and noticeable white stripes in the vivid pink. Its pungent leaves are somewhat fern like and the stems are often reddish. This is an erect many-stemmed plant.

Round-leaved Geranium
Geranium rotundifolium

Blooms	*Plant Height*	*Flower size*	*Origin*	*Life-form*
Mar-Aug	4-24 in	Small	Eur/N Afr/W Asia	Ann

This is an erect many-stemmed plant, common in Garland Ranch. Its flower is similar to that of the Cut-leaved Geranium *(G. dissectum)* but with a less intense color and a paler center. Its leaves are similar to the Dove's Foot Geranium but the tips of the younger leaves are more pointed and the segments of the maturer leaves have 5 lobes rather than 3.

Straggly Gooseberry
Ribes divaricatum var. *pubiflorum*

Blooms	Plant Height	Flower size	Origin	Life-form
Mar-May	3-9 ft	Medium	Native	Shrub

Far less common than the Fuchsia-flowered Gooseberry (*R. speciosum*), its stems are devoid of bristles although the nodes usually have 1-3 sharp spines. The sepals are green to purple and may be folded back like a Turk's Cap. The petals and filaments are white. The ovary and berry are without bristles.

Fuchsia-flowered Gooseberry
Ribes speciosum

Blooms	Plant Height	Flower size	Origin	Life-form
Dec-May	3-7 ft	Medium	Native	Shrub

A common deciduous, thorny shrub found in both shady and sunny areas, this produces beautiful fuchsia-like flowers in winter and spring. The fruit is edible, though the bristles make consumption somewhat challenging. The leaves turn bright red in late summer before dropping in the fall. Note the many stiff bristles along the stem.

Hillside Gooseberry
Ribes californicum var. *californicum*

Blooms	Plant Height	Flower size	Origin	Life-form
Mar-May	4-5 ft	Small	Native	Shrub

The flowers are similar to those of the Straggly Gooseberry, but the style has no hairs but the ovary (and fruit) are covered in short bristly hairs. The petals are white and the sepals usually red but may be green-tipped. The anthers are greenish-yellow. The young stems at least have no inter-nodal bristles.

Pink Flowering Currant
Ribes sanguineum var. *glutinosum*

Blooms	Plant Height	Flower size	Origin	Life-form
Feb-Apr	40-118 in	Small	Native	Shrub

Usually found in woodland, this large shrub has drooping clusters of 10-25 small pink to red flowers. The numerous glands on the rounded leaves have a strong musky fragrance. The blue to black fruit ripens towards fall but is dry and tasteless. The roots were once used as a remedy for toothache. There are no spines on the stems.

Giraffe Head
Lamium amplexicaule

Blooms	Plant Height	Flower size	Origin	Life-form
Jan-Sept	4-16 in	Med Clusters	Eurasia	Ann

This plant is found among the grass in the meadows and blooms in the spring and summer. It has long slender, bright red-purple tubular flowers that actually do look like the head and neck of a (strangely colored) Giraffe. The flowers and leaves are in whorls around the stems. Note that the leaves are sessile.

Red Henbit
Lamium purpureum

Blooms	Plant Height	Flower size	Origin	Life-form
Mar-Oct	4-24in	Medium	Europe	Ann

Not unlike the Giraffe Head *(L. amplexicaule)*, but the tubular flowers grow more or less horizontally and the leaves are larger with more pronounced lobes and have a distinct petiole. The flowers have beautiful Y-shaped orange stamens.

Pitcher Sage
Lepechinia calycina

Blooms	Plant Height	Flower size	Origin	Life-form
Apr-June	<80 in	Medium	Native	Per / Shrub

This is a largish shrub found in chaparral areas. The leaves are very similar to the Black Sage *(Salvia melllifera)* but the pendulous flowers, which may be either white or pale lavender are distinctive. Note how the four upper lips are rolled back and the larger lower lip is more extended. A very aromatic plant.

American Cornmint
Mentha canadensis *

Blooms	Plant Height	Flower size	Origin	Life-form
June-Oct	4-30 in	Med Clusters	Native	Per - rhizome

In Garland Ranch, this is found alongside or near water. Its flowers range from pale lilac to white and are found in whorled clusters along the stem. The aromatic leaves are lanceolate and serrated, with short hairs on the undersides and are smaller as they ascend the stem. The stem is noticeably hairy.

Coyote Mint
Monardella villosa ssp. *villosa*

Blooms	Plant Height	Flower size	Origin	Life-form
June-Aug	<20 in	Medium	Native	Subshrub

A common plant, sometimes low and straggly, sometimes in a bushy clump, this is usually found in open sun in mid summer. Its leaves are opposite and somewhat furry. When crushed, it has a pleasant fragrance.

Wood Mint / California Hedge-nettle
Stachys bullata

Blooms	Plant Height	Flower size	Origin	Life-form
Apr-Sept	16-30 in	Large Clusters	Native	Per

Sometimes known as Woundwort because of the antiseptic properties of its leaves, this is by far the commonest plant found in shady areas in Garland Ranch during the summer months. The leaves have a distinctive smell which some find attractive and others repellent.

Crimson Sage
Salvia spathacea

Blooms	Plant Height	Flower size	Origin	Life-form
Mar-May	12-24 in	Small	Native	Per

The flowers are 2-lipped with long exserted stigma and stamens. The wrinkled leaves are opposite and arrow shaped with rounded teeth on the margins and woolly beneath. The oval bracts and the stems are purplish-bronze colored, a pleasing contrast to the dark glowing red of the trumpet-shaped blossoms.

Grass Poly / Hyssop Loosestrife
Lythrum hyssopifolia

Blooms	Plant Height	Flower size	Origin	Life-form
Apr-Oct	6-20 in	Small	Eur #	Ann - S/L per

An uncommon plant in Garland Ranch though moderately invasive in certain areas, this is found in open disturbed areas, generally near water. It has inconspicuous pale pink flowers growing in leafy spikes, the leaves being narrow, upward pointing, oblong or elliptic and up to 1 inch long.

Cheeseweed
Malva parviflora

Blooms	Plant Height	Flower size	Origin	Life-form
Mar-Oct	8-30 in	Medium	Eur/Medit/India	Ann

Found at low elevations in grassy and disturbed areas, this plant is readily recognized by its rough and often folded leaves and its flat-topped fruit. The flowers are white to pinkish-blue. Note that the calyx is about the same length as the petal (unlike some other species of Mallow).

Checker Bloom
Sidalcea malviflora ssp. *malviflora*

Blooms	Plant Height	Flower size	Origin	Life-form
May-June	6-24 in	Large	Native	Per

Commonly found in open grassland, this unmistakable bright pink flower forms striking displays with other early summer bloomers such as Blue-eyed Grass and Johnny Jump-ups. The flowers range from pale to deep pink with 5 petals that have prominent veins and are squared off at the tip.

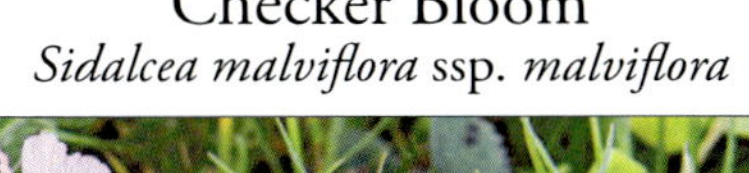

Red Maids
Calandrinia ciliata

Blooms	Plant Height	Flower size	Origin	Life-form
Mar-Aug	2-8 in	Medium	Native	Ann

This small bright pink flower is commonly found among other grassland flowers. Its intense color is unmistakable. It has long narrow leaves although its tendency to grow among other plants can give some misleading impressions of its true foliage. A white version is often seen.

Scarlet Pimpernel
Anagallis arvensis

Blooms	Plant Height	Flower size	Origin	Life-form
May-July	2-16 in	Medium	Eur	Ann

This is a contender for the most inappropriately named flower since the typical color is closer to orange than scarlet. It is very common in open sunny areas. It is also found in blue, pink and almost red forms. The flower is also known as the Poor Man's Weathervane. Optimistic Englishmen believed that if the flower opened in the morning, it would not rain that day. This is not the case.

Star Flower
Trientalis latifolia

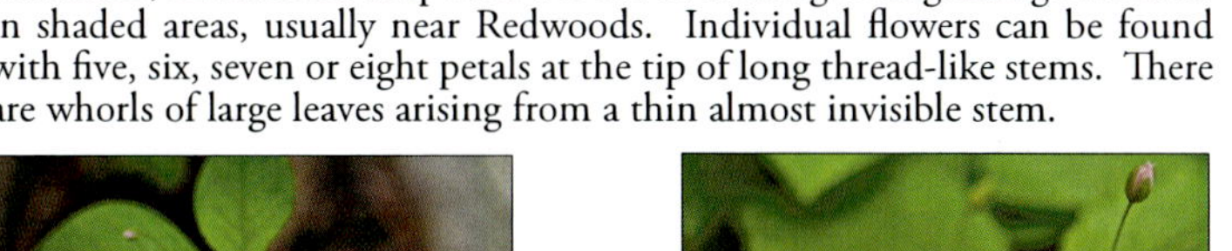

Blooms	Plant Height	Flower size	Origin	Life-form
Apr-June	2-6 in	Small	Native	Ann

This small, delicate star-shaped flower can be found growing in large numbers in shaded areas, usually near Redwoods. Individual flowers can be found with five, six, seven or eight petals at the tip of long thread-like stems. There are whorls of large leaves arising from a thin almost invisible stem.

Elegant Clarkia
Clarkia unguiculata

Blooms	Plant Height	Flower size	Origin	Life-form
Apr-Aug	24-30 in	Large	Native	Ann

This is very common, found in both sun and shade, a little after the appearance of the other Clarkias. The flowers grows in wheel-like fashion on tall stems, sometimes in spectacular large groups. Its typical color is dark pink with a deep crimson center, but it can also be found in salmon pink, red and even white forms.

Lewis' Clarkia
Clarkia lewisii

Blooms	*Plant Height*	*Flower size*	*Origin*	*Life-form*
May-Aug	<20 in	Large	Native	Ann

Although uncommon in California, this is present in abundance in Garland Ranch, often forming spectacular displays on sunny banks or open grassland. The base of the petals has a dark pink or red line and the lower part of the petals is almost white with pink speckles. The pendulous buds are also characteristic of the Lewis' Clarkia.

Winecup Clarkia / Four-Spotted Clarkia
Clarkia purpurea ssp. *quadrivulnera*

Blooms	*Plant Height*	*Flower size*	*Origin*	*Life-form*
May-July	6-18 in	Medium	Native	Ann

This is a very common Clarkia, found in late spring and early to mid summer in sunny areas, often in great numbers. The flowers are very variable in both color and appearance, ranging from pure deep maroon to pale pink with a darker heart-shaped blotch on each of the four petals.

Panicled Willow-herb
Epilobium brachycarpum

Blooms	Plant Height	Flower size	Origin	Life-form
Jun-Sept	8-80 in	Small	Native	Ann

This plant appears in open sunny dry areas in late summer with woody stems, a very open habit of growth and many small pink flowers. The petals are deeply cleft. Its seed pods have long pointed segments which pop open to reveal a central core which houses multiple seeds with fine white bristles.

California Willow-herb
Epilobium ciliatum ssp. *ciliatum*

Blooms	Plant Height	Flower size	Origin	Life-form
June-Sept	20-75 in	Small	Native	Per

This plant tends to grow in wet areas. It often forms clumps with longish lanceolate leaves and four-petalled pink flowers. Note how the petals are so deeply cleft that they appear almost as four pairs of petals. Note also the very distinctive oval seed pod and fine white bristles on the fruit.

California Fuchsia
Epilobium canum

Blooms	Plant Height	Flower size	Origin	Life-form
Aug-Nov	4-36 in	Large	Native	Per / Subshrub

This brilliant crimson or reddish-orange trumpet-shaped flower appears in late summer in open sunny positions. Its long stems have many narrow leaves which can be green to grayish-green. Also called hummingbird trumpet, the flower has 8 stamens which project well beyond the petals as does the pistil.

Striped Coralroot
Corallorhiza striata

Blooms	Plant Height	Flower size	Origin	Life-form
Feb-July	6-20 in	Large Cluster	Native	Per

This beautiful orchid has no leaves and, like other members of its genus, relies on symbiotic fungi in its coral-shaped roots for sustenance. It is found in the shade, typically (though not in Garland Ranch) in coniferous woodland. Although not uncommon further north, there was no record of this species having been seen in Monterey County before this plant was found in early 2011.

Pink Owl's Clover
Castilleja exserta ssp. *exserta*

Blooms	Plant Height	Flower size	Origin	Life-form
Mar-May	4-18 in	Med Cluster	Native	Ann

This is the most common form of Owl's Clover and is found in open grassy areas, frequently in profusion. It is broader than the Dense Flower Owl's Clover and can range in color from deep pink to white. Its profuse leaves are thread-like with 5-9 lobes and 10-50 mm long. The tips of the upper lips of the flowers are noticeably hairy without magnification and hooked.

Dense Flower Owl's Clover
Castilleja densiflora ssp. *densiflora*

Blooms	Plant Height	Flower size	Origin	Life-form
Mar-May	4-16 in	Med Cluster	Native	Ann

This less common form of Owl's Clover is found in open grassy areas and is distinguished by its taller and more slender flower spike. The leaves are linear to lanceolate, with 0-3 lobes and wider and longer (20-80 mm) and noticeably fewer in number than the Pink Owl's Clover *(C. exserta)*. The tips of the upper lips of the flowers are straight and not noticeably hairy.

Coast Paintbrush / Indian Paintbrush
Castilleja affinis ssp. *affinis*

Blooms	Plant Height	Flower size	Origin	Life-form
Mar-July	6-24 in	Med Cluster	Native	Per

Very commonly found, in sun or partial shade, the color of this flower varies from a reddish-orange to bright red. What appear to be red petals are in fact bracts (a form of leaf); the flowers are the thin green tubes (red on the underside) that extend out of the bracts. The plant is partially parasitic on the roots of grasses and other herbaceous plants.

Woolly Indian Paintbrush
Castilleja foliolosa

Blooms	Plant Height	Flower size	Origin	Life-form
Mar-July	6-24 in	Med Cluster	Native	Per

Easily mistaken for the Indian Paintbrush *(C. affinis)* this has a grayer appearance and noticeably woollier leaves and stems.

Both species are distinct from the Monterey Paintbrush (Seaside Painted Cup *(C. latifolia)* found by the coast.

Indian Warrior
Pedicularis densiflora

Blooms	Plant Height	Flower size	Origin	Life-form
Jan-Apr	2-22 in	Large Clusters	Native	Per

This is found in few places in Garland Ranch but in abundance when it is to be found, in the shade of shrubs and oaks. Its toothed bracts and tubular flowers are deep maroon (as compared to the scarlet of Indian Paintbrush). Its basal leaves are somewhat fern-like. Like Paintbrushes, it is parasitical on the roots of other plants, in this case, on Manzanita and other Ericaceae.

Fumitory
Fumaria officinalis

Blooms	Plant Height	Flower size	Origin	Life-form
Mar-May	8-24 in	Med Clusters	Eur	Ann

A plant commonly found in shady moist areas, this has a deep pink or purplish-red flower with purple tipped petals. There is a spur projecting from each flower. Traditionally considered to have medicinal properties but more recent sources warn that it may be poisonous if used incorrectly.

Sticky Snapdragon
Antirrhinum multiflorum

Blooms	Plant Height	Flower size	Origin	Life-form
May-June	2-5 ft	Large Clusters	Native	Ann - Per

Found on open slopes, this hairy, glandulous, sticky plant produces tall spikes of pink flowers. The spikes are 'racemose', i.e. producing flowers from the base upwards. The leaves are small and pointed, arranged alternately around the stem.

Scarlet Bugler
Penstemon centranthifolius

Blooms	Plant Height	Flower size	Origin	Life-form
Apr-June	12-48 in	Medium	Native	Per

Found in open grassy areas, each flower is a hanging fiery red tube about 1ft long with 5 fairly equal narrow lobes with small teeth at the ends. The blossoms droop from the same side of the tall, stiff, straight stem. The flower is similar to the California Fuchsia *(Epilobium canum)* but simpler. Its flowering season is earlier and its upright growth habit is very different.

Chaparral Gilia
Gilia angelensis

Blooms	Plant Height	Flower size	Origin	Life-form
Mar-May	3-28 in	Very Small	Native	Ann

Found in open sunny areas, this very small Gilia flowers in loose clusters with the petals varying from lavender to white, sometimes with a yellowish throat. The purple stripes on the calyx help to identify this species.

Purplespot Gilia
Gilia clivorum

Blooms	Plant Height	Flower size	Origin	Life-form
Mar-May	2-12 in	Very Small	Native	Ann

Found in open grassland, this tiny Gilia has distinct purplish spots at the base of the petals and a yellow throat (though this is very hard to detect given the size of the flower). It is very hard to spot once the grass starts growing vigorously. The calyx and stem are very hairy.

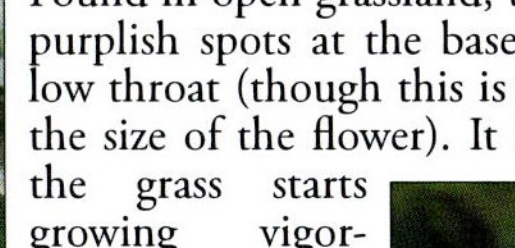

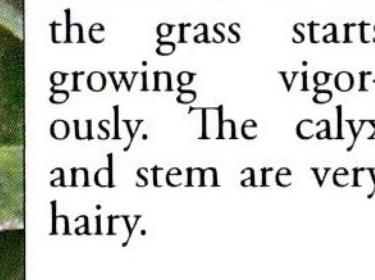

Slender-flowered Gilia
Gilia tenuiflora ssp. *tenuiflora*

Blooms	Plant Height	Flower size	Origin	Life-form
Apr-June	6-16 in	Small	Native	Ann

Found in open sunny areas, this produces multiple flowers on wide-spreading stems. The flowers are about twice the size of those of the Chaparral and Purplespot Gilias and are also distinguished by their dark purple, long, slender tubes/throats. The rest of the petal is pinkish violet or light blue.

Tricolor / Bird's Eye Gilia
Gilia tricolor ssp. *tricolor*

Blooms	Plant Height	Flower size	Origin	Life-form
Mar-June	4-16 in	Small	Native	Ann

Found in open sunny areas, this might at first sight be mistaken for the Chaparral Gilia and its flowers are a similar size. The three colors (a pale lemon throat, purple spots merging into a ring and very pale violet/blue petals) are distinctive. The purple ring is especially visible on the outside of the petals. Not previously known at Garland Ranch, this may have been recently introduced.

Slender Phlox
Microsteris gracilis *

Blooms	Plant Height	Flower size	Origin	Life-form
Mar-Aug	<8 in	Small	Native	Ann

A low growing plant, sometimes tuft-like, sometimes erect. The leaves are lance shaped, opposite at the lower end of the stem, alternate at the top. They are glandular and hairy. The tiny flowers are delicate, five-petalled and pale pink with a white center. It is more likely to be found in the early part of its flowering season.

California Milkwort
Polygala californica

Blooms	Plant Height	Flower size	Origin	Life-form
Apr-June	2-14 in	Small	Native	Per

The only member of its family to be found in Monterey County, this is found in chaparral or exposed slopes. Its flowers are somewhat pea-like but its two wing petals open almost flat and tend to droop when the flower is fully open. The lower petal is shaped like a keel with a small blunt tip, or beak, which is yellow.

Douglas' Spine-flower
Chorizanthe douglasii

Blooms	Plant Height	Flower size	Origin	Life-form
Apr-July	4-20 in	Small Clusters	Native	Ann

This plant comes in several distinct forms. Some are very low growing and compact, found in exposed areas on or beside trails; others bear clusters of flowers at the end of much longer branching stems and are found among other plants on exposed hillsides. The triangular involucre is very distinctive, the flowers themselves are more rounded.

Turkish Rugging
Chorizanthe staticoides

Blooms	Plant Height	Flower size	Origin	Life-form
Apr-July	2-24 in	Small Clusters	Native	Ann

At first sight, this looks quite like Douglas' Spine-flower (*C. douglasii*), but the flowers are quite distinct, with three larger rounded petals alternating with three smaller ones. Note the rosy stems. It typically grows very low to the ground in exposed areas on or by the side of trails at higher elevations.

Long-stemmed & Naked Buckwheat
Eriogonum elongatum & Eriogonum nudum var. *auriculatum*

Blooms	Plant Height	Flower size	Origin	Life-form
Aug-Oct	30-70 in	Small Clusters	Native	Per

These are both much-branched plants. The Long-stemmed (L) has flower heads located at the nodes of its white felty stems. The Naked (R) has small clusters only in the axils or at the tips of its bare (sometimes felty) stems. Leaves are mostly basal on the Long-stemmed. The Naked has wavy leaves only low on the stem; upper stems are bare. Found in dry rocky places.

California Buckwheat
Eriogonum fasciculatum var. *foliolosum*

Blooms	Plant Height	Flower size	Origin	Life-form
Mar-Oct	4-60 in	Small Clusters	Native	Shrub

This is a common shrub, found in dry sunny areas. Its flowers are in tight clusters at the end of stems and at the stem nodes. The leaves of this species are distinctive, growing in a fasciculate fashion, i.e. in clusters. While many buckwheats have similar flowers they have widely varying leaves and growth habits.

Saint Catherine's Lace
Eriogonum giganteum

Blooms	*Plant Height*	*Flower size*	*Origin*	*Life-form*
June-Sept	1-12 ft	Large Clusters	Native	Shrub

This large Buckwheat has large flower heads with an umbel-like appearance. It is most easily distinguished by its thick grayish felty leaves. The individual flowers are less densely packed in the flower heads than with most of the other Buckwheats. This is found by the edges of the main parking lot.

Slender Woolly Buckwheat & Elegant Buckwheat
Eriogonum gracile var. *gracile* & *Eriogonum elegans*

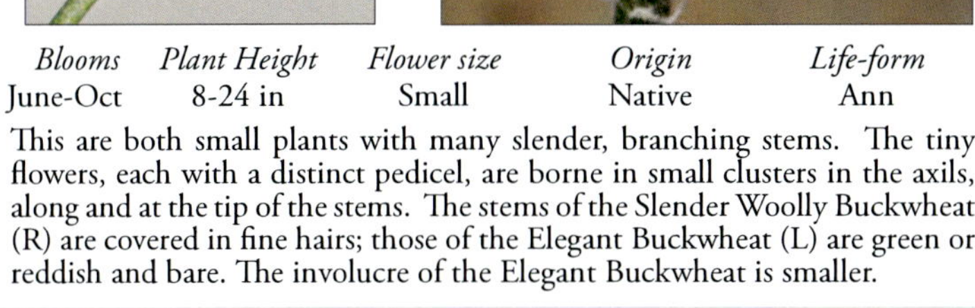

Blooms	*Plant Height*	*Flower size*	*Origin*	*Life-form*
June-Oct	8-24 in	Small	Native	Ann

This are both small plants with many slender, branching stems. The tiny flowers, each with a distinct pedicel, are borne in small clusters in the axils, along and at the tip of the stems. The stems of the Slender Woolly Buckwheat (R) are covered in fine hairs; those of the Elegant Buckwheat (L) are green or reddish and bare. The involucre of the Elegant Buckwheat is smaller.

Sheep Sorrel
Rumex acetosella

Blooms	Plant Height	Flower size	Origin	Life-form
Feb-May	<16 in	Very Small	Eur / Asia ##	Per

A moderately invasive weed, found in open grassland, this appears at first sight as a nondescript brownish red plant of no great interest. A close examination of the flowers show them to be of surprising complexity and beauty. It belongs to the same genus as the Docks.

Padre's Shooting Star
Dodecatheon clevelandii ssp. *sanctarum*

Blooms	Plant Height	Flower size	Origin	Life-form
Feb-Apr	5-18 in	Large	Native	Per

A contender for the most beautiful flower of all; this appears in very large numbers in open areas in the early spring. The color ranges from dark lavender through light lavender to pure white, all the same species. The leaves are basal forming a neat rosette. The name 'shooting star' derives from the way in which the petals flare backwards like the tail of a comet.

Protea
Protea sp.

Blooms	Plant Height	Flower size	Origin	Life-form
May-June	<8 ft	Large	S Africa	Shrub

A native of South Africa (of which it is the national flower), this impressive flower is to be found near the Mesa where it was planted (with other specimens which have not survived) by the owners before Garland Ranch became a regional park.

Crimson Columbine
Aquilegia formosa

Blooms	Plant Height	Flower size	Origin	Life-form
Apr-Aug	8-30 in	Large	Native	Per

This dramatic flower is extremely uncommon in Garland Ranch but is quite unmistakable when seen. Each of the 5 petals forms a long hollow tube slanting backwards from the long hanging golden yellow stamens. Between the petal tubes are the petal-like spreading sepals. Found in moist areas.

Red Larkspur
Delphinium nudicaule

Blooms	Plant Height	Flower size	Origin	Life-form
Mar-June	6-22 in	Large	Native	Per

This appears to grow in only one place in Garland Ranch, near one of the footbridges on the Redwood Canyon Trail where a number of plants may be found growing on a vertical rock face. The reddish flowers are unmistakeable with their long wavy spurs. The leaves are large with broad lobes.

California Wild Rose
Rosa californica

Blooms	Plant Height	Flower size	Origin	Life-form
May-Aug	30-100 in	Large	Native	Shrub

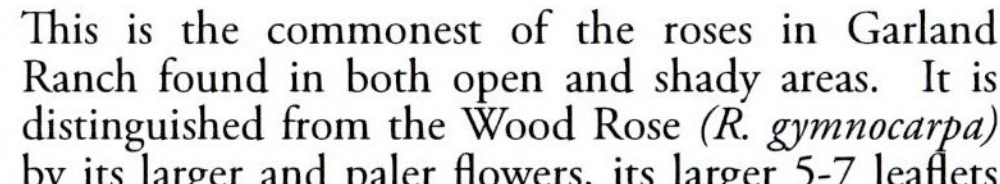

This is the commonest of the roses in Garland Ranch found in both open and shady areas. It is distinguished from the Wood Rose *(R. gymnocarpa)* by its larger and paler flowers, its larger 5-7 leaflets and by its down curving stout prickles. Its sepals are 'persistent', i.e. they remain on the hip.

Wood Rose
Rosa gymnocarpa var. *gymnocarpa*

Blooms	Plant Height	Flower size	Origin	Life-form
May-June	20-80 in	Medium	Native	Loose Shrub

Although not as common as the California Rose *(R. californica)*, this is often found in more shaded areas. Its smaller flowers are usually deep pink and its leaflets (up to 9 in number) also are smaller. It has numerous prickles which are slender and straight. Its sepals are 'deciduous', i.e. they fall off the hip. The pistils (in the very center of the flower) number 5-10 (in contrast to the Pine Rose).

Pine Rose
Rosa pinetorum

Blooms	Plant Height	Flower size	Origin	Life-form
May-June	<40 in	Medium	Native	Dwarf Shrub

A small rose, very uncommon in Garland Ranch; usually found among pines. Its flowers are pink to deep red. Its prickles are straight. It is similar to the Wood Rose, although the flower is larger (petals being 5-20 mm rather than 10 mm), the hips retain their sepals, leaflets are 7 or fewer and the pistils (in the very center of the flower) and more numerous (10-20) and congested.

Bee Plant / Coast Figwort
Scrophularia californica

Blooms	Plant Height	Flower size	Origin	Life-form
Feb-June	40-72 in	Small	Native	Per

A common plant found mainly but not only in shade; it has a single square stem and serrated leaves, quite large at the base but progressively smaller towards the top of the stem. It has many very small deep crimson flowers which produce copious nectar and, as its common name suggests, are attractive to bees.

Pink Plectritis
Plectritis congesta ssp. *brachystemon*

Blooms	Plant Height	Flower size	Origin	Life-form
Mar-June	0-20 in	Small Cluster	Native	Ann

Fairly common in open slopes and grassy places, where it can appear in profusion, this plant produces small heads with tiny white to pink flowers (each 1.5 - 3.5 mm across). Each of the flowers has a spur which may be a small swelling or slender and about 1/3 the length of the petal. *P.c.* ssp. *congesta* is similar but larger, with pale to dark pink flowers 4 - 9.5 mm across.

Blue Elderberry
Sambucus nigra ssp. *caerulea* *

Blooms	Plant Height	Flower size	Origin	Life-form
Mar-Sept	7-25 ft	Large Clusters	Native	Shrub / Tree

An unmistakable large shrub with its large dense clusters of creamy-white flowers and dusty blue berries (sometimes appearing simultaneously). The ripe berries can be eaten but they are poisonous when unripe as is much of the rest of the plant.

Laurustinus
Viburnum tinus

Blooms	Plant Height	Flower size	Origin	Life-form
Oct-Mar	>20 ft	Large Clusters	Medit	Shrub

This might at first sight be thought to be a Dogwood, but its clusters of flattened white five-petalled flowers are distinctively different and the leaves are more similar to a Laurel (hence the common name).

This may be a garden escapee; it appears not to grow naturally in the wild in California. The small berries are blue.

Soap Plant
Chlorogalum pomeridianum var. *pomeridianum*

Blooms	Plant Height	Flower size	Origin	Life-form
May-Aug	24-30 in	Medium	Native	Bulb

This is a common plant with long slightly wavy basal leaves and comparatively long flower stems. Each stem can produce multiple flowers which do not open until mid to late afternoon and close before morning. The fibrous bulb was used by the Native Americans in a variety of ways.

Yucca / Our Lord's Candle
Hesperoyucca whipplei *

Blooms	Plant Height	Flower size	Origin	Life-form
May-Aug	1-13 ft	Large Clusters	Native	Bulb

This magnificent plant is uncommon in Garland Ranch, growing mainly by the Manzanita Trail in Kahn Ranch. It has a rosette of large, narrow, gray-green leaves and a very large, dense panicle of beautiful creamy-white flowers. The plant takes many years to reach maturity and dies after fruiting although it produces offshoots from the base which develop into new plants.

Bur Chervil
Anthriscus caucalis

Blooms	Plant Height	Flower size	Origin	Life-form
Apr-June	18-40 in	Large Clusters	Eurasia	Ann

A common shade-loving plant, this has very feathery leaves and umbels of small white flowers which produce small hooked burs which give the plant its common name.

Poison Hemlock
Conium maculatum

Blooms	Plant Height	Flower size	Origin	Life-form
Apr-June	2-10 ft	Large Clusters	Eur ##	Bienn

This is a moderately (in some areas highly) invasive species which readily colonizes open spaces. Its leaves and flowers are similar to the Bur Chervil but it can be distinguished partly by its size and partly by the reddish blotches (known as 'Socrates' blood') on its stems. All parts of this plant are poisonous.

Cow Parsnip
Heracleum maximum *

Blooms	Plant Height	Flower size	Origin	Life-form
Mar-July	3-10 ft	Large Clusters	Native	Per

The plant is strong smelling, stout and found in moist, shady places. The 6-16 inch leaves are compound in 3 divisions, toothed and deeply lobed and cause blisters and/or rashes if rubbed. There are broad swellings at the junction of the leaf stalk and plant stem. Note the umbels (up to 12 inches) of small, dull white flowers, each with 5 notched petals.

Shepherd's Needle
Scandix pecten-veneris

Blooms	Plant Height	Flower size	Origin	Life-form
Mar-June	6-14 in	Small Clusters	Medit	Ann

Found in grassland or disturbed places, this plant has primary and secondary umbels with 2-5 conspicuous bractlets beneath the secondary umbel of tiny white flowers. When the flowers go to seed, the resulting clusters of narrow pointed fruit resemble side-by-side or spreading needles, hence the common name. Note the parsley-like leaves.

Wood Sweet Cicely
Osmorhiza berteroi *

Blooms	Plant Height	Flower size	Origin	Life-form
Apr-June	12-48 in	Small	Native	Per

The two Sweet Cicelys are common shade loving plants with long peduncles ending in loose compound umbels of tiny flowers. Their leaves are less finely toothed than the Bur Chervil. The Wood Sweet Cicely has white flowers with no subtending bracts and its fruits are slender with a long pedicel.

California Sweet Cicely
Osmorhiza brachypoda

Blooms	Plant Height	Flower size	Origin	Life-form
Mar-May	12-30 in	Small	Native	Per

Less common than the Wood Sweet Cicely *(O. berteroi)*, this has compound umbels with greenish-yellow flowers subtended by noticeable bracts which remain visible even after the fruits develop. The pedicels are much shorter than those of the Wood Sweet Cicely and the fruits are slightly shorter and fatter.

Field Hedge Parsley
Torilis arvensis

Blooms	Plant Height	Flower size	Origin	Life-form
Apr-July	12-40 in	Small	C & S Eur ##	Ann

Another common shade loving plant; this can easily be confused with Sweet Cicely *(Osmorhiza chilensis)* but its leaves are narrower and more serrated and its fruits form small roundish burs; the hairs of which (unlike some other hedge parsleys) appear only on one side of the fruit.

Knotted Hedge Parsley
Torilis nodosa

Blooms	Plant Height	Flower size	Origin	Life-form
Apr-June	4-28 in	Small	Eurasia	Ann

Although the plant appears similar to the Field Hedge Parsley *(T. arvensis)*, the flowers grow in small round clusters at the nodes on the stem rather than on the end of a long pedicel, and the fruits have hairs on all sides.

Indian Milkweed
Asclepias eriocarpa

Blooms	Plant Height	Flower size	Origin	Life-form
June-Sept	16-30 in	Medium	Native	Ann

Found in sunny areas, this is very distinctive with its woolly gray leaves and its clusters of creamy white flowers with a pink tinge. The Monarch butterflies are particularly attracted to it and it was used by the indigenous peoples for medicinal purposes (e.g. to treat rattlesnake bites) and as a source of fibre.

California Milkweed / Narrow-leaved Milkweed
Asclepias fascicularis

Blooms	Plant Height	Flower size	Origin	Life-form
June-Sept	16-30 in	Medium	Native	Ann

Found in dry, sunny meadows, this has many small flowers, typically pink, but sometimes white or purplish, borne in clusters at the end of erect stems. The long, thin leaves are borne in whorls of 3 to 6. The milkweeds have milky sap from which Thomas Edison attempted but failed to make rubber.

Elk Clover
Aralia californica

Blooms	Plant Height	Flower size	Origin	Life-form
June-Aug	12-36 in	Med Clusters	Native	Per

This belongs to the same family as the non-native Ivy (e.g. *Hedera helix*) and has similar flowers. It thrives in damp conditions and is noticeable more for its very large leaves (individual leaflets can be as much as 12 in long) than its undistinguished greenish-white flowers borne in small spherical clusters.

Coltsfoot
Petasites frigidus var. *palmatus*

Blooms	Plant Height	Flower size	Origin	Life-form
Feb-Mar	<16 in	Med Cluster	Native	Per

Found in damp areas by stream beds, this produces a single flowering stem with a head of small white flowers. The flower stem appears in early spring before the distinctive, large (6-8 in) palmate leaves with their 5-6 deeply cleft segments and shallow lobes.

Common Yarrow
Achillea millefolium

Blooms	Plant Height	Flower size	Origin	Life-form
Mar-Oct	4-80 in	Large Clusters	Native	Per

Very common, both in sun and part shade, this has dense flat-topped clusters of small pure white flowers and long feathery leaves. The very tiny disk flowers are white. It is very attractive to butterflies. The species name means thousand-leaved referring to its fern-like strongly scented leaves.

Mugwort
Artemisia douglasiana

Blooms	Plant Height	Flower size	Origin	Life-form
June-Oct	2-8 ft	Very Small	Native	Per

More easily recognized by its aromatic leaves than its small and undistinguished flowers, Mugwort is best known as an antidote to Poison Oak. Since Poison Oak is far more common than Mugwort, avoidance is unquestionably better than reliance on the antidote. The underside of the leaf is white which helps differentiate it from Nettles.

Mayweed / Dog Fennel
Anthemis cotula

Blooms	Plant Height	Flower size	Origin	Life-form
Apr-Aug	4-24 in	Medium	Eur ##	Ann

Not very common in Garland Ranch, this likes open sunny places. The ray flowers turn back with age and sometimes drop off leaving only the yellow disk flowers looking like very rounded Brass Buttons *(Cotula coronopifolia)* (though these are not found in Garland Ranch). The feathery leaves are distinctive.

Rough-leaved Aster
Eurybia radulina *

Blooms	Plant Height	Flower size	Origin	Life-form
July-Oct	8-28 in	Medium	Native	Per

Uncommon in Garland Ranch, this plant is found in shady areas, and has rather strappy white ray flowers, yellow to orange disk flowers and longish, broad toothed leaves which are rough to the touch.

Marsh Baccharis
Baccharis glutinosa *

Blooms	Plant Height	Flower size	Origin	Life-form
June-Oct	< 6ft	Small	Native	Per

Usually found in or near moist areas, this plant has a a herbaceous appearance, in contrast to the shrubby Mule Fat *(B. salicifolia)*, the stems being woody only near the base. The leaves are ovate to lanceolate. Like Coyote Brush and Mule Fat, the Marsh Baccharis is dioecious with male (lower R) and female (upper R) flowers being borne on different plants.

Mule Fat
Baccharis salicifolia ssp. *salicifolia*

Blooms	Plant Height	Flower size	Origin	Life-form
May-June	>12 ft	Small	Native	Shrub

Usually found near water, this medium to large shrub has long slender willow-shaped leaves but can be distinguished from Willow by its small fuzzy flowers. Like the Coyote Brush *(B. pilularis)*, the plant is dioecious. The long straight stems of this shrub form excellent drills for use when making fire the old-fashioned way.

Coyote Brush
Baccharis pilularis ssp. *consanguinea*

Blooms	Plant Height	Flower size	Origin	Life-form
Aug-Dec	>3 ft	Small	Native	Shrub

A very common evergreen shrub found in scrub or chaparral, this has small tough leaves and produces a mass of small creamy flowers. The plant is 'dioecious', i.e. the (longer, more slender, white) female and the (shorter, more rounded, creamy-yellow) male flowers are borne on separate plants.

Horseweed
Erigeron canadensis *

Blooms	Plant Height	Flower size	Origin	Life-form
June-Sept	<80 in	Very Small	Native	Ann

A very common plant of open sunny areas, this has many long narrow leaves growing up its stem and in late summer produces a mass of tiny, inconspicuous white flowers. It is more easily recognized by its shape than by its flowers. It has a close relative, the South American Conyza (*E. bonariensis*), which is shorter and, like Groundsel, has only disk flowers.

White-flowered Hawkweed
Hieracium albiflorum

Blooms	Plant Height	Flower size	Origin	Life-form
June-Aug	16-30 in	Medium	Native	Per

Common in shade or part shade, this is sometimes confused with California Chicory (*Rafinesquia californica*) but it has fewer ray flowers and its leaves are very different, mostly basal, hairy and without serration or indentations. The stems likewise are covered with coarse hairs and have milky sap.

California Chicory
Rafinesquia californica

Blooms	Plant Height	Flower size	Origin	Life-form
Apr-June	8-60 in	Medium	Native	Ann

Commonly found in shade or part shade, this has very distinctive, coarsely indented or toothed leaves and outward curving phyllaries. Note the reddish stripe on the outside of some of the ray flowers.

Pearly Everlasting
Anaphalis margaritacea

Blooms	Plant Height	Flower size	Origin	Life-form
June-Aug	8-48 in	Small	Native	Per subshrub

Easily mistaken for California Cudweed (*Pseudognaphalium californicum*), this blooms later in the year but can be distinguished with certainty by the underside of its leaf which is whitish and hairy unlike the smooth green of the California Cudweed. The leaves are also not decurrent. The bracts are white.

California Cudweed / California Everlasting
Pseudognaphalium californicum *

Blooms	Plant Height	Flower size	Origin	Life-form
Mar-June	8-33 in	Small	Native	Ann - Per

Very common in many environments, this strongly aromatic plant is often mistaken for Pearly Everlasting (*Anaphalis margaritacea*). It is however far more common, blooms earlier in the year and its leaves are smooth and green on both sides. Note also that the leaves are 'decurrent', i.e. the leaf base extends down the stem from the apparent point of insertion.

Fragrant Everlasting
Pseudognaphalium beneolens *

Blooms	Plant Height	Flower size	Origin	Life-form
July-Oct	8-43 in	Small	Native	Ann - S/L per

This is found in open areas, usually near water and, despite its name, has no or only a very slight fragrance. This species can be distinguished from the White Everlasting (*P. microcephalum*) by its more narrow 'decurrent' upper leaves (i.e. the leaf base extending down the main stem) and its gray-green color versus the white color and hairy flowers of the White Everlasting.

Pink Everlasting
Pseudognaphalium ramosissimum *

Blooms	Plant Height	Flower size	Origin	Life-form
June-Sept	6-48 in	Small	Native	Bienn

Commonly found in open areas, this is usually a tall plant which has a distinctively loose but many-branched growth habit. Its leaves are green, top and bottom, narrow and without wool. The small flowers are mostly pink or pinkish-white or, rarely, yellow.

Weedy Cudweed
Pseudognaphalium luteoalbum *

Blooms	Plant Height	Flower size	Origin	Life-form
Jan-Dec	4-24 in	Small	Eurasia	Ann

Very common in waste places, this could be confused with Cotton-batting Plant *(P. stramineum)* but it has a more slender growth pattern and the flowers have reddish tips. The leaves are woolly on both surfaces.

Cotton-batting Plant
Pseudognaphalium stramineum *

Blooms	Plant Height	Flower size	Origin	Life-form
June-Oct	3-27 in	Small	Native	Ann - bienn

Found in moist disturbed places, this plant is usually covered with densely-woven, matted hairs throughout and unscented. The longish slender leaves are decurrent (appearing to continue down the stem) and are woolly on both surfaces. The heads are in dense terminal clusters with yellow tips.

Lowland Cudweed & Purple Cudweed
Gnaphalium palustre & Gamochaeta ustulata *

Blooms	Plant Height	Flower size	Origin	Life-form
LC: Aug-Oct	<6 in	Small	Native	Ann
PC: Apr-July	4-16 in	Medium	Native	Ann

These are two of the less distinctive cudweeds; both with flower heads clustered at the tips of the stems. The Lowland Cudweed (above) has pale yellow flowers and the leaves surmount the flower heads which are covered in cobwebby hairs. It is now the only Gnaphalium in California.

The Purple Cudweed (left) has spoon-shaped to oblanceolate leaves and small clusters of very undistinguished purplish flowers.

Slender Cottonweed
Micropus californicus var. *californicus*

Blooms	Plant Height	Flower size	Origin	Life-form
Apr-June	<6 in	Very small	Native	Ann

This is a grayish-white cobwebby plant often covered with densely woven matted hairs. Found in large patches in dry or moist, bare or grassy areas. The heads are 3-4 mm. The flowers heads are in clusters of 4-6, 5-lobed with tiny disk flowers. Also called the 'Q-tip plant'.

Tejon Cryptantha
Cryptantha microstachys

Blooms	Plant Height	Flower size	Origin	Life-form
Apr-June	<6 in	Very Small	Native	Ann

Found in open sun, the most characteristic features of this Cryptantha are its tiny size flowers (0.5-3.0 mm), the bristly hairs and bristles on the stem and the finer hairs surrounding the blooms.

Cleveland's Cryptantha / Common Cryptantha
Cryptantha clevelandii var. *florosa*

Blooms	Plant Height	Flower size	Origin	Life-form
Apr-June	4-24 in	Small	Native	Ann

A very small Cryptantha, this has hairy stems and very small white flowers with a pale yellow center. The Cryptanthas can be extremely hard and sometimes impossible to distinguish with the naked eye.

Rusty Popcorn Flower
Plagiobothrys nothofulvus

Blooms	Plant Height	Flower size	Origin	Life-form
Mar-May	8-28 in	Small	Native	Ann

The most common of the popcorn flowers in Garland Ranch, this grows in great profusion in open grasslands. The leaves are mostly basal with some arranged alternately up the stem. The flowers are pure white, sometimes with a pale yellow center. The common name comes from the rusty colored calyx.

Small-flowered Nemophila
Nemophila parviflora var. *parviflora*

Blooms	Plant Height	Flower size	Origin	Life-form
Apr-June	<3 in	Very small	Native	Ann

Appropriately named, this plant has tiny flowers, less than 3mm in diameter. It is to be found in shady areas and its hairy, lobed leaves are quite distinctive. The flowers may be white or blue (in which case they resesemble a tiny Baby Blue Eyes); only the white ones have been observed in Garland Ranch.

Common Phacelia
Phacelia distans

Blooms	Plant Height	Flower size	Origin	Life-form
Mar-June	6-30 in	Small	Native	Ann

The flowers and leaves of the Common Phacelia are similar to those of the Branching Phacelia *(P. ramosissima)* but the plant is smaller and, if branching at all, only at the base. Note the pinnate leaves with clearly toothed segments which come up to the inflorescence. The flowers may be white or blue.

Stinging Phacelia
Phacelia malvifolia

Blooms	Plant Height	Flower size	Origin	Life-form
Apr-June	8-39 in	Small	Native	Ann

The most common of the Phacelias in Garland Ranch, its toothed maple-like leaves are covered in stiff glandular hairs which can produce a noticeable sting when touched. The blooms appear at the end of a curving or coiled cyme (i.e. a structure on which the terminal flowers appear first).

California Phacelia
Phacelia egena

Blooms	Plant Height	Flower size	Origin	Life-form
May-June	6-24 in	Small	Native	Per

This is very similar to the Imbricate Phacelia (*P. imbricata*) (though slightly smaller) with similar bell-shaped flowers and the same narrow, pointed leaves. Note however that the calyx lobes along the flower head are clearly separated whereas those on the Imbricate Phacelia overlap each other.

Imbricate Phacelia
Phacelia imbricata ssp. *imbricata*

Blooms	Plant Height	Flower size	Origin	Life-form
May-June	8-48 in	Small	Native	Per

This Phacelia is most easily recognized by the fact that its flowers tend to be more cylindrical than bell shaped and by its leaves which are narrow and pointed with several pairs of smaller leaves immediately below the terminal leaf. Note the overlapping ("imbricate"= tile-like) calyx lobes.

Milk Maids / California Toothwort
Cardamine californica

Blooms	*Plant Height*	*Flower size*	*Origin*	*Life-form*
Feb-May	8-28 in	Medium	Native	Per

One of the commonest shade-loving plants found in the early spring, this has clusters of pure white (occasionally pale rose) flowers. The leaves are variable, from narrow and arrow shaped through broad to rounded, sometimes with very small lobes and sometimes with very distinct ones.

Bitter Cress
Cardamine oligosperma

Blooms	*Plant Height*	*Flower size*	*Origin*	*Life-form*
Mar-June	4-15 in	Very small	Native	Ann

Found on shady banks, creek bottoms and wet meadows, this has tiny four-petalled flowers. Note the linear seed pods (0.75-1.50 in) similar to those seen in the other mustards. The upper cauline leaves are much narrower than the lower ones.

Shepherd's Purse
Capsella bursa-pastoris

Blooms	Plant Height	Flower size	Origin	Life-form
Mar-June	16-48 in	Small	Eurasia	Ann

A very common plant in grassland and scrub, it has a small cluster of white flowers with purple tipped sepals and very distinctive roughly heart shaped fruits. When ripe the seedpod splits down the middle, releasing the yellow seeds referred to as the 'golden coins' in the shepherd's purse.

Common Peppergrass
Lepidium nitidum

Blooms	Plant Height	Flower size	Origin	Life-form
Feb-Apr	4-16 in	Very Small	Native	Ann

The flowers are tiny, white and arranged in clusters at the end of the stems which branch near the base. Note the flattened, shiny, oval seedpods with the slight notch and a seam down the middle and borne on a slightly flattened pedicel. The pods turn red to maroon as they age.

Hairy Fringe Pod
Thysanocarpus curvipes

Blooms	Plant Height	Flower size	Origin	Life-form
Mar-May	6-30 in	Very Small	Native	Ann

This is very commonly found in open grassland. The very small flowers appear in a cluster at the top of the stem, the spent flowers lower down the stem turning into very distinctive oval fruits, which sometimes have a ring of small perforations around the rim, not unlike a miniature sand dollar. Note the "auriculate" leaf, clasping but not quite surrounding the stem.

Narrow-leaved Fringe Pod
Thysanocarpus laciniatus

Blooms	Plant Height	Flower size	Origin	Life-form
Mar-May	6-30 in	Very Small	Native	Ann

This is very similar to the Hairy Fringe Pod (*T. curvipes*) and is believed to hybridize with it. Note however that the leaves are much narrower and do not clasp the stem in the same way as those of the Hairy Fringe Pod. The fruits often have wavy ("crenellated") edges and are not perforated like those of the Hairy Fringe Pod.

Watercress
Nasturtium officinale *

Blooms	Plant Height	Flower size	Origin	Life-form
Mar-Nov	4-24 in	Small	Native	Per

Commonly found in or by streams in dense mats, this is reputed to be one of the oldest leaf vegetables consumed by human beings. It has small 4-petalled white flowers and narrow straight or upcurving seed pods. The leaves have a peppery taste.

Tower Mustard
Turritis glabra *

Blooms	Plant Height	Flower size	Origin	Life-form
Mar-June	16-48 in	Small	Native	Bienn

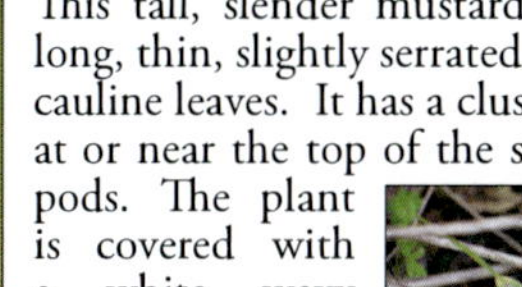

This tall, slender mustard has a single stem with long, thin, slightly serrated basal leaves and alternate cauline leaves. It has a cluster of small white flowers at or near the top of the stem. Note the erect seed pods. The plant is covered with a white waxy substance which rubs away.

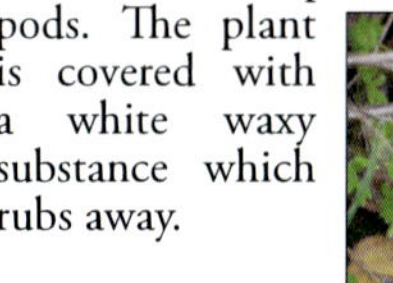

Field Chickweed & Mouse-ear Chickweed
Cerastium arvense ssp. *strictum* & *Cerastium glomeratum*

Blooms	Plant Height	Flower size	Origin	Life-form
Mar-May	3-18 in	Small	Native	Per

The native Field Chickweed, with its broad slightly lobed petals is distinguishable from the more common (and alien) Common Chickweed (opposite) and Mouse-ear Chickweed (*C. glomeratum*) (R) by prominent veins on the petals and larger flowers.

Common Chickweed
Stellaria media

Blooms	Plant Height	Flower size	Origin	Life-form
Mar-June	1-16 in	Small	SW Eur	Ann

This chickweed is a low growing plant with very small white flowers. Its 5 petals are split down the middle making them look like 10 instead of 5 and so distinguishable from the less lobed flowers of the Field and Mouse-ear Chickweeds (opposite); note also the hairs confined to one side of the stem.

Douglas' Sandwort
Minuartia douglasii

Blooms	Plant Height	Flower size	Origin	Life-form
April-June	2-12 in	Small	Native	Ann

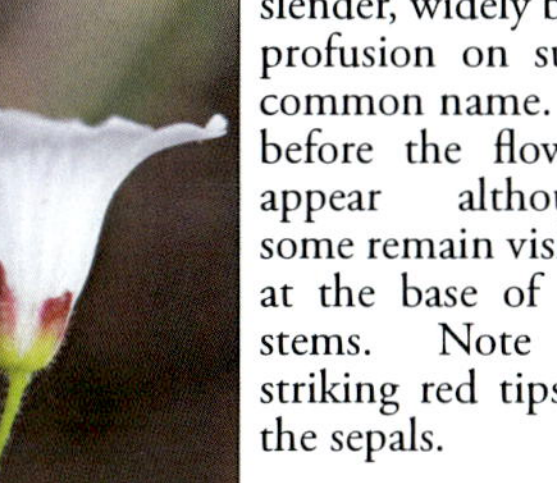

This charming little bell-shaped flower grows on slender, widely branching, stems. It is found in some profusion on sunny, often sandy slopes, hence its common name. Most of its thread-like leaves die off before the flowers appear although some remain visible at the base of the stems. Note the striking red tips of the sepals.

Spurry / Starwort
Spergula arvensis ssp. *arvensis*

Blooms	Plant Height	Flower size	Origin	Life-form
Mar-June	4-16 in	Small	Eur	Ann

This is a fairly common low growing plant, found in open grassy areas. It has a distinctive five petalled shape with sepals alternating behind and between each petal to create the star pattern which gives the plant one of its common names. Note the whorled, linear leaves, and the 5-lobed stigma.

Windmill Pink / Catchfly
Silene gallica

Blooms	Plant Height	Flower size	Origin	Life-form
Apr-Oct	4-16 in	Small	Eur	Ann

This is a very common plant found in open sunny areas throughout the late spring and early summer. The hairy, bladder-shaped calyx with its purplish striped veins is very distinctive. The common name appears to come from the sticky hairs on the calyx which can catch small insects.

Lemmon's Campion / Lemmon's Catchfly
Silene lemmonii

Blooms	Plant Height	Flower size	Origin	Life-form
June-Aug	6-18 in	Medium	Native	Per

This is an unusual species of Catchfly which can be found in partly shaded areas. It has strikingly beautiful flowers which may be either white with a green bladder-shaped calyx or pink with a pink bladder. Note the long, exserted stamens.

Field Bindweed
Convolvulus arvensis

Blooms	Plant Height	Flower size	Origin	Life-form
May-Oct	8-12 in	Large	Eur	Per

Bindweed is a Morning-glory. It is better found in the field than in one's garden in view of its tendency to spread aggressively. It has white to pink-flecked flowers, spade-shaped leaves and bracts on the stem well below the flower. The stigma are noticeably linear and cleft in this species.

Hill Morning-glory
Calystegia subacaulis ssp. *subacaulis*

Blooms	Plant Height	Flower size	Origin	Life-form
Apr-June	1-8 in	Large	Native	Per

Less commonly found is the Hill or Stemless Morning-glory which is very low growing and produces its flowers with little if any stem. The leaves are roughly triangular with rounded backward lobes, unlike the very pointed lobes typical of some other morning glories. Bracts are equal to but do not conceal the calyx.

Coast Morning-glory
Calystegia macrostegia ssp. *cyclostegia*

Blooms	Plant Height	Flower size	Origin	Life-form
Mar-Aug	>100 in	Large	Native	Per

This is an extremely common and aggressive vine with beautiful pink-flecked white funnel-shaped flowers. Note the calyx is enclosed or closely subtended by a pair of large sepal-like bracts. Leaves are triangular.

Purple-striped Morning-glory
Calystegia purpurata ssp. *purpurata*

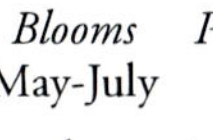
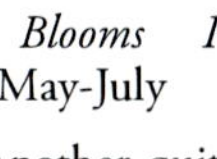
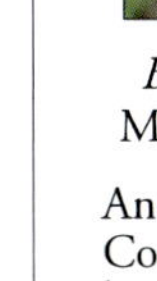

Blooms	Plant Height	Flower size	Origin	Life-form
May-July	> 3ft	Large	Native	Per

Another quite common Morning-glory, this can easily be mistaken for the Coast Morning Glory. It can however be distinguished by the small, leaf-like bract a little below the calyx in contrast to the sepal-like bracts of the Coast Morning glory which usually enclose the calyx. Note also the deep "V" at the base of the leaves.

Wild Cucumber
Marah fabacea

Blooms	Plant Height	Flower size	Origin	Life-form
Mar-Apr	[Vine]	Small	Native	Per

This is a very common and aggressive vine which produces small (usually 5-petalled) cream to-white flowers in the spring followed by large and very prickly fruit a little later in the year. The female flowers appear singly and are noticeably larger than the male flowers. The plant is sometimes known as Manroot because of the remarkable size and shape of the roots on old plants.

Western Red Dogwood
Cornus sericea ssp. *occidentalis*

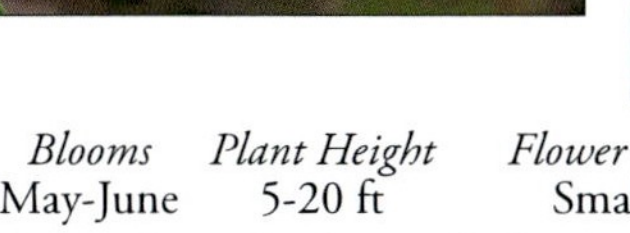

Blooms	Plant Height	Flower size	Origin	Life-form
May-June	5-20 ft	Small	Native	Shrub

This is a large shrub, usually found alongside streams. It has clusters of small cruciform flowers and whitish berries, sometimes at the same time. It has 4-7 veins in its leaves, unlike the similar Brown Dogwood (*C. glabrata*) which has 3-4. The mature stems are noticeably red.

Madrone
Arbutus menziesii

Blooms	Plant Height	Flower size	Origin	Life-form
Mar-May	[Tree]	Large Clusters	Native	Tree

The Madrone is a large tree with large roundish ovate leaves. It bears clusters of small white flowers in spring which turn into glorious displays of red berries in the late fall. Its bark peels away from the trunk leaving bare the characteristic reddish wood. Although dense, the wood cracks easily and is not good for woodworking.

Manzanita - Shaggy Barked & Toro
Arctostaphylos tomentosa & Arctostaphylos montereyensis

Blooms	Plant Height	Flower size	Origin	Life-form
Jan-Mar	3-8 ft	Med Clusters	Native	Shrub

These two Manzanitas have similar flowers. The Shaggy-Barked Manzanita (L) has flaking bark that gives it its name and leaves that are green above but have whitish felt-like hairs underneath. The Toro (or Monterey) Manzanita (R) has more erect, smoother leaves, though they feel rough on the edges and underneath, and it lacks the burls found on the Shaggy-barked Manzanita.

Turkey Mullein
Croton setigerus *

Blooms	Plant Height	Flower size	Origin	Life-form
May-Oct	0-8 in	Small	Native	Ann

A low growing plant sometimes prostrate, sometimes in low mounds, found in grassland; it has distinctive felty gray-green leaves and very small and rather undistinguished white flowers. The seeds are attractive to wild turkeys and other birds, hence its common name. Also known as Doveweed.

Nuttall's Locoweed / Nuttall's Milkvetch
Astragalus nuttallii var. *nuttallii*

Blooms	Plant Height	Flower size	Origin	Life-form
Jan-Oct	8-39 in	Med Cluster	Native	Ann

This is found in grassland. It has 25 small oval leaflets and produces clusters of milky white flowers which then turn into inflated pods, pale green on the underside and pinkish above. Toxins produced by the Locoweed family are poisonous to livestock; hence its common name.

Coast Silk Tassel
Garrya elliptica

Blooms	Plant Height	Flower size	Origin	Life-form
Jan-Apr	<24 ft	Large Clusters	Native	Shrub / Sm Tree

This is a large shrub or small evergreen tree with tough leaves green on top but paler underneath. It is dioecious, with male and female flowers appearing on separate trees. The gray-green male catkins (R) form showy cascades; the female (L) are shorter and more of a silver-gray. The fruits are hairy. Because of the seeds they contain, the female flowers are firm to the touch.

Horehound
Marrubium vulgare

Blooms	Plant Height	Flower size	Origin	Life-form
May-June	4-24 in	Med Clusters	Eur #	Per

Common in waste places, this has whorls of small white flowers and a mint's characteristic square stems. It has noticeably gray to greenish-gray wrinkled, ovate leaves and is typically low growing and spreading but with some taller stems. It has been used to make a tea which serves as an expectorant and to make hard lozenges to aid digestion and soothe sore throats.

Black Sage
Salvia mellifera

Blooms	Plant Height	Flower size	Origin	Life-form
Apr-June	40-100 in	Medium	Native	Shrub

A very common shrub found in scrub and chaparral, this has long, narrow and highly aromatic leaves and whorled clusters of tubular whitish flowers separated by about an inch of stem. The common name refers to the blooms that remain after they set seed forming dark spheres along the dry stems.

Yerba Buena
Clinopodium douglasii *

Blooms	Plant Height	Flower size	Origin	Life-form
Apr-Sept	<4 in	Small	Native	Per

A very common but easily overlooked small herb, this has delicate white flowers and fresh smelling minty leaves that (as the name, derived from the Spanish for 'good herb', suggests) have both medicinal and culinary properties (principally as an infusion).

Fairy Lantern / Globe Lily
Calochortus albus

Blooms	Plant Height	Flower size	Origin	Life-form
Apr-June	8-31 in	Medium	Native	Bulb

This beautiful flower is very common in full or part shade. It has delicate creamy-white flowers and a distinctive three-sided seed pod. Before the flowers appear, its location can be identified by its single, long strap-like leaf lying prostrate on the ground. The flowers hang from the slender stems like a lantern. The yellow hump is a nectar gland.

Fairy Bells
Prosartes hookeri *

Blooms	Plant Height	Flower size	Origin	Life-form
Mar-May	12-30 in	Medium	Native	Per - Rhizome

A shade lover, this not uncommon plant has very delicate pale green to cream, bell shaped flowers hanging down below the leaves. In late summer, the fruit appears as orange to bright red berries. The leaves could be mistaken for the Fat or Slim Solomon but they are smaller and their branching growth habit is quite distinct.

Narrow-leaved Flax
Linum bienne

Blooms	Plant Height	Flower size	Origin	Life-form
Apr-Aug	8-40 in	Small	Eurasia	Bienn / per

Found in open grassland, this delicate white to pale blue flower, sometimes with a very pale pink rim, appears in mid summer and can be found in great profusion. The flowers are short-lived. Note the very narrow leaves which remain close to the stem near its top.

Fremont's Star Lily
Toxicoscordion fremontii *

Blooms	Plant Height	Flower size	Origin	Life-form
Mar-May	16-36 in	Large Clusters	Native	Bulb

A fairly common early spring flower, this produces large clusters of white star-shaped flowers in loose spikes. It has long, narrow basal leaves. It is sometimes known as Fremont's Death Camas, since all parts of the plant are poisonous. It is found on grassy or bushy slopes and at the edge of trails.

Miner's Lettuce
Claytonia perfoliata ssp. *perfoliata*

Blooms	Plant Height	Flower size	Origin	Life-form
Feb-May	4-16 in	Small	Native	Ann

Found everywhere in shade or part shade, this has very small white flowers, initially singly very close to the large roundish leaf and later in the season in twos or threes or more at the end of a stem. A related species, the Small-flowered Claytonia (*C. parviflora*) (lower R) has more flowers and less obviously perforated leaves.

Red-stemmed Spring Beauty
Claytonia rubra ssp. *depressa*

Blooms	Plant Height	Flower size	Origin	Life-form
Mar-June	<6 in	Small	Native	Ann

Far less common than Miner's Lettuce, this is recognizable by its red stems and leaves; elliptical basal leaves and fused cauline leaves whose shape resembles two Miner's Lettuce leaves joined together. The multitude of flowers fully justifies the plant's common name.

Elegant Rein-orchid
Piperia elegans ssp. *elegans*

Blooms	Plant Height	Flower size	Origin	Life-form
June-July	6-28 in	Small	Native	Per

Uncommon in Garland Ranch, this, like the Michael's Rein-orchid *(P. michaelii)*, has a down-curving spur but, unlike it, has pure white flowers, often with green veins, borne in greater profusion. Specimens found by the coast tend to have more flowers than those found further inland.

Michael's Rein-orchid
Piperia michaelii

Blooms	Plant Height	Flower size	Origin	Life-form
July-Aug	6-28 in	Small	Native	Per

Listed in the CNPS Inventory of Rare and Endangered Plants, this is found in several locations in Garland Ranch. It has slender lanceolate leaves and a tall stem with pale green flowers. They can be distinguished from other species by the broad spade-shaped lower lip and the long, down-curving spur.

Transverse Rein-orchid
Piperia transversa

Blooms	Plant Height	Flower size	Origin	Life-form
June-July	6-22 in	Medium	Native	Per

This elegant shade-loving flower appears in mid summer. It is recognizable by its long straight spurs that extend horizontally from the flower. By comparison, the long spur of the Elegant Rein-orchid *(P. elegans)* is curved downwards and its flowers are more densely clustered.

Narrow-leaved Owl's Clover
Castilleja attenuata

Blooms	Plant Height	Flower size	Origin	Life-form
Apr-June	4-20 in	Large Clusters	Native	Ann

This has long (20-80 mm) narrow leaves with 0-3 lobes, similar to the Dense Flower Owl's Clover *(C. densiflora)* and the ends of its bracts are either white or yellow with its flowers being white with yellow or purple dots.

Cream Cups
Platystemon californicus

Blooms	Plant Height	Flower size	Origin	Life-form
Mar-May	4-12 in	Medium	Native	Ann

Found in open sun, this delicate flower typically has cream petals with a yellow base although the appearance can be quite variable. The globular shape of the half-opened flower is distinctive as are the hairy stems. This species can be difficult to distinguish from the Narrow-leaved Meconella (*Hesperomecon linearis*).

Coulter's Matilija Poppy
Romneya coulteri

Blooms	Plant Height	Flower size	Origin	Life-form
May-Oct	3-8 ft	Large	Native	Subshrub/Shrub

This spectacular poppy is a large perennial sub-shrub with silvery green, deeply cut leaves. The large pure white, wrinkled petals and the flower's bright yellow center are unmistakable; the largest flower of any member of the poppy family. It is a native of Santa Barbara County.

California Plantain
Plantago erecta

Blooms	Plant Height	Flower size	Origin	Life-form
Mar-May	1-12 in	Very small	Native	Ann

This tiny plant has white flowers with a deep red center, very fine silky hairs and exserted stamens, almost none of which would be visible to someone standing up. There are short, rounded flowering spikes and linear leaves, quite different from the invasive English Plantain.

Cut-leaved Plantain
Plantago coronopus

Blooms	Plant Height	Flower size	Origin	Life-form
June-Aug	2-20 in	Medium	Eur	Ann-bienn

A common plantain, found in open and waste areas, this has distinctive slender, pinnately lobed, lanceolate leaves. The flowers form spikes at the end of long curved stems forming a crown shape - hence the scientific name of the species.

English Plantain & Common Plantain
Plantago lanceolata & Plantago major

Blooms	Plant Height	Flower size	Origin	Life-form
Apr-Aug	8-30 in	Medium	Eur	per

Very common in grassland and scrub areas, the English Plantain has distinctive erect to spreading lanceolate leaves and a tight cone-shaped spike surrounded by a circlet of tiny white flowers.

The Common Plantain has leaves that are typically broadly elliptic, spreading out close to the ground. The flowers are unremarkable.

Western Virgin's Bower
Clematis ligusticifolia

Blooms	Plant Height	Flower size	Origin	Life-form
June-Aug	[Vine]	Medium	Native	Vine

Not uncommon in Garland Ranch, this is found mainly at lower levels, climbing in shrubs or trees. It produces large numbers of delicate star shaped flowers and very hairy fruits which, in quantity, provide a spectacular display and give the plant one of its other common names, Old Man's Beard.

Bicolored Linanthus
Leptosiphon bicolor *

Blooms	Plant Height	Flower size	Origin	Life-form
Mar-June	2-6 in	Small	Native	Ann

This very small Linanthus is found in open sun. It is less than one centimeter across and has a yellow throat. The petals range from white to pink. The styles and stamen are not as exserted and the stigma much shorter than those in the Common Linanthus (*L. parviflorus*). Only one flower is generally open at a time.

Common Linanthus
Leptosiphon parviflorus *

Blooms	Plant Height	Flower size	Origin	Life-form
Apr-June	2-10 in	Small	Native	Ann

This is the more common of the Linanthus in Garland Ranch, slightly larger than the Bicolored Linanthus (*L. bicolor*). The throat is usually yellow but can also be very deep maroon. Note the whorled leaves and long, exserted stigma. The petals are usually white but pink forms are not uncommon.

Buck Brush
Ceanothus cuneatus var. *cuneatus*

Blooms	Plant Height	Flower size	Origin	Life-form
Jan-May	>10 ft	Small Clusters	Native	Shrub

This large shrub is found in chaparral, producing a profusion of clusters of very small flowers which range in color from pure white to very pale blue or lavender. It has small, tough, one-veined oval leaves.

California Coffeeberry
Frangula californica ssp. *californica* *

Blooms	Plant Height	Flower size	Origin	Life-form
Apr-June	<18 ft	Small Clusters	Native	Shrub / Sm Tree

This large shrub bears clusters of small creamy white flowers which turn into red and then black berries. The berries have strong and potentially dangerous laxative effects. The leaves are smooth-edged or barely serrated (in contrast to Toyon). The Hoary Coffeeberry (*F.c.* ssp. *tomentella* *) (lower R) is very similar but for its leaves which are pale and slightly hairy underneath.

Redberry / Spiny Redberry
Rhamnus crocea

Blooms	Plant Height	Flower size	Origin	Life-form
Mar-Apr	<7 ft	Small	Native	Shrub

This shrub produces masses of small creamy-green flowers which turn into very shiny red berries in the summer. The name derives from the sometimes thorny tips to the rigid branches. The berries are smaller and the leaves are much smaller and tougher than those of the California and Hoary Coffeeberry (*Frangula californica*).

Toyon / Christmas Berry
Heteromeles arbutifolia

Blooms	Plant Height	Flower size	Origin	Life-form
June-Aug	<17 ft	Large Clusters	Native	Shrub / Sm Tree

A common large shrub found in many habitats, this is most easily identified by its pointed and serrated leaves. It produces a mass of attractive white flowers in the summer followed by berries which turn from green to bright red towards the end of the year, so giving the plant one of its common names.

Chamise
Adenostoma fasciculatum var. *fasciculatum*

Blooms	Plant Height	Flower size	Origin	Life-form
July-Aug	>13 ft	Large Clusters	Native	Shrub / Sm Tree

This large shrub is very common in the chaparral. It has clusters of small narrow pointed leaves (the 'fascicles' which give the plant its Latin name) and a mass of tiny white flowers which produce a spectacular display in the mid summer months turning whole ridges a uniform white.

Cream Bush / Ocean Spray
Holodiscus discolor var. *discolor*

Blooms	Plant Height	Flower size	Origin	Life-form
May-Aug	5-20 ft	Large Clusters	Native	Shrub

A large loose growing shrub, this produces large panicles of small, creamy white flowers, usually in the late spring and early summer. Its roundish lobed leaves are very distinctive. Found in woods and rocky places.

Leafy Horkelia
Horkelia californica var. *frondosa*

Blooms	Plant Height	Flower size	Origin	Life-form
May-Sept	4-48 in	Medium	Native	Per

This plant, with its hairy, toothed leaves and white 5-petalled flowers, can be difficult to distinguish from the Sticky Cinquefoil (*Drymocallis glandulosa*), but close examination shows that it has only 10 stamens whereas the Sticky Cinquefoil typically has 20 or more. The California Horkelia (*H. californica*) is similar but its sepals are red flecked (not just rimmed) on the inside.

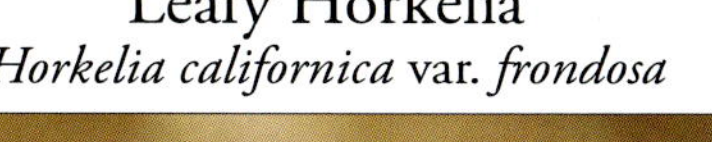

Sticky Cinquefoil
Drymocallis glandulosa ssp. *wrangelliana* *

Blooms	Plant Height	Flower size	Origin	Life-form
May-June	2-36 in	Medium	Native	Per

This is a common flower, found in sun or part shade. Its flowers vary from bright yellow to creamy white, the latter being the form typically found in Garland Ranch. The flowers are more open, have many more stamens (20 or more) and have more rounded petals than those of the California Horkelia.

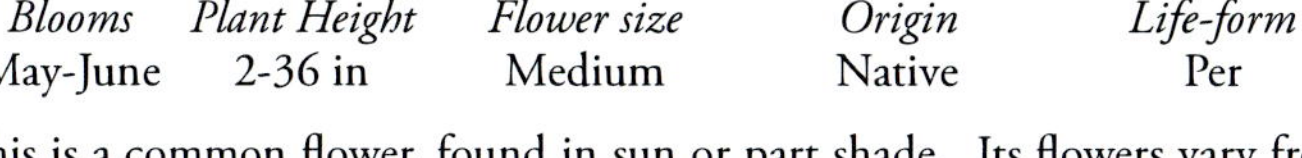

Oso Berry / Indian Plum
Oemleria cerasiformis

Blooms	Plant Height	Flower size	Origin	Life-form
Feb-Apr	3-17 ft	Small	Native	Shrub / Sm Tree

This is a large fragrant shrub with an open flowing growth pattern. It produces small hanging clusters of white bell-shaped flowers and blue-black bean-shaped fruits in the fall. The fruits are said to be edible but no guarantees are offered as to their flavor. It is dioecious, with male and female flowers normally borne on separate plants.

Western Choke Cherry
Prunus virginiana var. *demissa*

Blooms	Plant Height	Flower size	Origin	Life-form
Apr-May	<20 ft	Large Clusters	Native	Shrub / Sm Tree

This is a very large shrub or small tree which produces long racemes of creamy white flowers. The fruit is edible but bitter-tasting. The leaves are highly toxic. Usually found in shady woodland and canyons and on shady slopes but also tolerates open sun.

Holly-leaved Cherry
Prunus ilicifolia ssp. *ilicifolia*

Blooms	Plant Height	Flower size	Origin	Life-form
Apr-May	7-30 ft	Med Clusters	Native	Shrub/ SmTree

Its broadly ovate laves have spiny serrations reminiscent of the Holly and may be mistaken for Coast Live Oak leaves. When crushed the leaves give off an unmistakable almond scent. It has clusters of white flowers, about 5 cm long, followed by large-stoned purple fruit later in the summer.

Wood Strawberry
Fragaria vesca

Blooms	Plant Height	Flower size	Origin	Life-form
May-June	1-12 in	Medium	Native	Per

This ever-popular plant needs little introduction save to say that its fruits make up in flavor for what they lack in size. The Latin name for strawberry was *fraga*, derived from *fragum*, meaning fragrant, a clear reference to the unmistakable sweet smell as well as taste of the fruit. Note the three-part leaves and gleaming white blossoms.

Thimbleberry
Rubus parviflorus

Blooms	Plant Height	Flower size	Origin	Life-form
May-Aug	40-80 in	Large	Native	Shrub

This is a very common bush, found in shady areas, especially near water. It has large leaves and beautiful and unmistakable white flowers, much larger than the scientific name would suggest. Its fruit looks like a slightly flat raspberry and is hard to photograph because of the temptation to eat it first.

California Blackberry
Rubus ursinus

Blooms	Plant Height	Flower size	Origin	Life-form
Feb-June	>6 ft	Medium	Native	Shrub

Very common aggressively rambling vine with spiny stems, this has attractive and quite variable white flowers and edible fruit in the fall. Although the plant grows equally happily in shade and part sun, the fruit is best when it has been exposed to the sun. Note the rough spade-shaped leaf.

Fat Solomon / False Solomon's Seal
Maianthemum racemosum *

Blooms	Plant Height	Flower size	Origin	Life-form
Mar-May	12-36 in	Med Cluster	Native	Per - rhizome

A very common shade-loving plant, this produces a dense cluster of white flowers at the tip of the stem. The berries are first green, then yellow, then dull red with purple speckles. Its alternate large leaves are very distinctive.

Slim Solomon
Maianthemum stellatum *

Blooms	Plant Height	Flower size	Origin	Life-form
Mar-May	12-28 in	Med Cluster	Native	Per - rhizome

This is less common than the Fat Solomon (*M. racemosa*). Its flowers are in looser clusters and the individual flowers have a simple star shape that gives the plant its Latin name.

The berries are green with three distinct dark stripes, turning red later in the summer.

Climbing Bedstraw & Goose Grass
Galium porrigens var. *porrigens* & *Galium aparine*

Blooms	Plant Height	Flower size	Origin	Life-form
May-June	[Vine]	Small	Native	Per

This is a very common vine, usually found climbing in or around other shrubs. It has creamy star-shaped flowers and longish ovate leaves in whorls of 4, both flowers and leaves often tinged red. A similar plant is Goose Grass (*G. aparine* (L)) with leaves in whorls of 6-8. All cling readily to clothes.

California Buckeye
Aesculus californica

Blooms	Plant Height	Flower size	Origin	Life-form
May-June	12-40 ft	Large Cluster	Native	Tree

This is a very common, large deciduous tree. Like the Horse Chestnut, it produces large showy white flowers in the spring followed by a large nut covered in a thick felty skin. It loses its leaves very early, in mid-summer. The name apparently derives from native American folklore which noted the resemblance of the nut to the eye of the male deer.

Woodland Star
Lithophragma affine

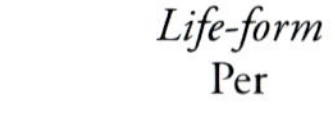

Blooms	Plant Height	Flower size	Origin	Life-form
Mar-May	4-24 in	Small	Native	Per

The Woodland Star is a beautiful spring flower found in shaded areas. It has long delicate red or green stems, often with an abundance of blooms. It is easily confused with the more common Hill Star (*L. heterophylla*) but note the tapered calyx which is clearly distinctive.

Hill Star
Lithophragma heterophyllum

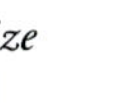

Blooms	Plant Height	Flower size	Origin	Life-form
Mar-June	4-20 in	Small	Native	Per

The Hill Star is another beautiful spring flower found in shaded areas, very similar to the Woodland Star (*L. affine*) but much more common in Garland Ranch. It can be distinguished by the square end of its calyx as opposed to the tapered calyx of the Woodland Star. The flowers are indistinguishable.

Brook Foam
Boykinia occidentalis

Blooms	Plant Height	Flower size	Origin	Life-form
June-July	8-24 in	Small	Native	Per

This is found on the face of waterfalls or by streams. It has distinctive indented, spade-shaped leaves and small clusters of open bell-like white flowers on long, branching stems.

Small-flowered Alum Root
Heuchera micrantha

Blooms	Plant Height	Flower size	Origin	Life-form
May-June	4-39 in	Very Small	Native	Per

Found in shade areas, sometimes in the middle of trails, this has distinctive leaves (similar to those of other members of the Heuchera genus), large with noticeable dark veins and a tall branching stem bearing many tiny white and pink flowers.

California Saxifrage
Micranthes californica *

Blooms	Plant Height	Flower size	Origin	Life-form
Feb-June	4-12 in	Small	Native	Per

This plant grows mainly in shade or part shade, in great profusion in the early Spring. It has a basal rosette of hairy leaves and a single long, branching red flower stem. Note the delicate white flowers with 5 rounded petals with 10 stamens with bright pink anthers. The flowers grow in clusters.

Tolguacha
Datura wrightii

Blooms	Plant Height	Flower size	Origin	Life-form
Apr-Oct	20-60 in	Large	Native (Mexico?)	Ann-Per

Similar to Jimson Weed (*D. stramonium*) but the leaves are felty in appearance and with a strong, sweet smell. The large, trumpet shaped flowers are also similar except that the margins of the flowers are folded back. The fruit is broadly similar but hanging rather than erect and more spherical than egg-shaped. Both plants are hallucinogenic and highly toxic.

Douglas' Nightshade
Solanum douglasii

Blooms	*Plant Height*	*Flower size*	*Origin*	*Life-form*
June-Dec	<80 in	Small	Native	Per/Subshrub

This straggling shade-loving plant produces its small white flowers (in loose umbels) throughout much of the year. The bright yellow anthers stand together at the center of the flower with almost no filaments, and form a cylinder around the style. In the summer and fall it bears green berries that turn black. They are poisonous if eaten.

Indian Tobacco
Nicotiana quadrivalvis

Blooms	*Plant Height*	*Flower size*	*Origin*	*Life-form*
May-Oct	12-79 in	Large	Native	Ann

These are long slender trumpet-like white flowers with long petals. Leaves are oblong to oval with the blade portion extending to the base of the petiole. The flower is 4-7 cm long and gradually widening from its base. The plant is glandular, hairy and ill smelling.

Sweet Fennel
Foeniculum vulgare

Blooms	Plant Height	Flower size	Origin	Life-form
May-Sept	36-84 in	Large Clusters	S Eur ###	Per

This is a highly invasive species, unmistakable with its large umbelliferous heads and yellow flowers. Its feathery leaves are also distinctive and valued for their culinary properties. They are a primary ingredient of absinthe and have a licorice aroma.

Caraway-leaved Lomatium
Lomatium caruifolium

Blooms	Plant Height	Flower size	Origin	Life-form
Mar-May	6-18 in	Med Clusters	Native	Per

Like all Lomatiums there are large umbelliferous heads of yellow flowers. It can most easily be identified by its highly cut leaves which, as the name suggests, resemble Caraway or Fennel leaves. Note the red 'wings' of the fruit which are narrower than the greenish body. Found in wet, grassy areas.

Small-leaved Lomatium
Lomatium parvifolium

Blooms	Plant Height	Flower size	Origin	Life-form
Mar-June	6-16 in	Med Clusters	Native	Per

This is a comparatively unusual Lomatium, most easily distinguished by its leaves with their broad pointed teeth (with small spines at the tip) although the shape of the leaves is variable. The leaflets are more or less separated. The fruit have broad wings and are notched at the apex.

Common Lomatium
Lomatium utriculatum

Blooms	Plant Height	Flower size	Origin	Life-form
Feb-May	4-20 in	Med Clusters	Native	Per

As the name suggests, this is commonly found in both sun and part shade. Its leaves are both basal and cauline, deeply cut and finely divided though not as much as in the Carawayleaf Lomatium *(L. caruifolium)*. Note the broad wings of the fruit, usually broader than the body.

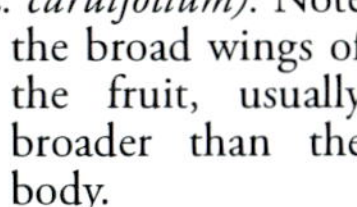

Footsteps of Spring
Sanicula arctopoides

Blooms	Plant Height	Flower size	Origin	Life-form
Mar-June	0-2 in	Medium	Native	Bienn

Appropriately named, for it is one of the first flowers to bloom, making greenish-yellow mats of color on the hillsides as grass is just beginning to show. The prickly looking yellow-green leaves are much divided. The species name means 'bear's foot' in Greek.

Hartweg's Tauschia
Tauschia hartwegii

Blooms	Plant Height	Flower size	Origin	Life-form
Mar-May	12-40 in	Med Clusters	Native	Per

Easily mistaken for a Lomatium (because of its flowers) or Gambleweed (because of its leaves), this is fairly common in shaded areas. It has distinctive leaves subdivided into five leaflets with rounded, toothed segments.

Gambleweed / Pacific Sanicle
Sanicula crassicaulis

Blooms	*Plant Height*	*Flower size*	*Origin*	*Life-form*
Mar-June	9-48 in	Medium	Native	Per

A very common shade-loving plant, this has noticeable lobed or serrated leaves and multiple heads of small yellow flowers with backward curving petals. Each flower head has about 5 pointed bracts at its base. The umbels are not well developed as in the Lomatiums. Its fruits form small burs.

Poison Sanicle
Sanicula bipinnata

Blooms	*Plant Height*	*Flower size*	*Origin*	*Life-form*
Mar-June	4-24 in	Medium	Native	Per

Much lesss common than Gambleweed, this has slender pinnate and lobed leaves. Like Gambleweed, its flowers are in small clusters often surrounded by small leaves. Although the leaves have a coriander-like smell, they are better not eaten since the plant is toxic, though only mildly so.

Large-flowered Agoseris / Giant Dandelion
Agoseris grandiflora var. *grandiflora*

Blooms	Plant Height	Flower size	Origin	Life-form
Mar-June	10-33 in	Large	Native	Per

This large flower is most easily identified by its many, long, narrow basal leaves and by its long tapered buds with their red-streaked phyllaries, the lower ones being short and reflexed. Another distinctive characteristic is the fruit, with a ribbed body and the beak (joining the body and the plumose tips) typically being twice as long as the body itself.

Annual Agoseris
Agoseris heterophylla var. *heterophylla*

Blooms	Plant Height	Flower size	Origin	Life-form
Apr-June	2-16 in	Medium	Native	Ann

A much smaller plant and flower than its large-flowered relative (opposite), this has lanceolate basal leaves. Unlike many other members of the Sunflower family, but like all other members of the Dandelion "tribe" the Agoseris has ligules (like ray flowers but bisexual).

Woodland Madia
Anisocarpus madioides *

Blooms	Plant Height	Flower size	Origin	Life-form
Apr-Sept	6-30 in	Medium	Native	Per

Another shade-loving Madia, this has fewer heads than the Slender Tarweed (*Madia gracilis*) and the buds are more rounded in shape. It has 7-15 ray flowers. The anthers may be yellow or brown. Most distinctive, however, are the opposite leaves, especially on the lower part of the stem.

Coast Tarweed
Deinandra corymbosa *

Blooms	Plant Height	Flower size	Origin	Life-form
May-Oct	8-39 in	Medium	Native	Ann

Very common by the coast and occasionally found in Garland Ranch, this has 18-35 ray flowers and is thus easily distinguished from its namesake (Coast Tarweed (*Madia sativa*)) which has only 8-13 ray flowers. Its upper leaves are very slender and crowded below the inflorescence; the lower leaves are usually lobed.

California Brickellbush
Brickellia californica

Blooms	Plant Height	Flower size	Origin	Life-form
Aug-Oct	20-80 in	Medium	Native	Shrub

Uncommon in Garland Ranch, this will be found growing near the Carmel River. It is a moderate-sized, many-branched shrub with small oval to spade-shaped leaves, some alternate and some opposite. It has bunches of narrow flowers with extruding filament-like greenish-yellow disk flowers. Its overlapping phyllaries are green with a purple tinge.

Tocalote / Maltese Star Thistle
Centaurea melitensis

Blooms	Plant Height	Flower size	Origin	Life-form
Apr-Aug	4-39 in	Medium	S Eur ##	Ann

This is a moderately invasive thistle with prominent dark-purple spine-tipped phyllaries and bright yellow flowers, not to be confused with the Yellow Star Thistle (*C. solstitialis (R)*) which has fewer but much longer, pale yellow spines but is not found in Garland Ranch. Tocalote's short, narrow grayish-green leaves are soft and can be handled with impunity. Bachelor's Button (*C. cyanus*) (L) belongs to the same genus. This is occasionally seen at Garland Ranch.

Mock Heather
Ericameria ericoides

Blooms	Plant Height	Flower size	Origin	Life-form
Aug-Nov	<40 in	Med Clusters	Native	Shrub/subshrub

A common shrub found in open sunny areas, this produces a mass of small slightly untidy looking flowers with 2-6 ray flowers and 8-14 disk flowers. Its grayish leaves are almost cylindrical and the axillary leaves form small fan-shaped clusters. It tends to form a much smaller plant closer to the Coast.

Sawtooth Goldenbush
Hazardia squarrosa

Blooms	Plant Height	Flower size	Origin	Life-form
Aug-Oct	12-90 in	Medium	Native	Shrub

This can be a fairly tall upright shrub found in scrub and chaparral. It has tough serrated leaves and yellow 'discoid' flowers; i.e. flower heads with only disk flowers with yellow stamens and no ray flowers. Its recurved (backward curving) phyllaries are thick, with green tips.

Golden Fleece
Ericameria arborescens

Blooms	Plant Height	Flower size	Origin	Life-form
Aug-Nov	<10 ft	Small Clusters	Native	Shrub/subshrub

At first sight, this might be mistaken for the Western Goldenrod, both having many narrow leaves and clusters of small bright yellow flowers. Note however that the Golden Fleece is a large shrub with loose spreading branches, prefers open chaparral and has only disk flowers. Its leaves have a sharp tips. Its common name derives from the woolly appearance of its fruits.

Western Goldenrod
Euthamia occidentalis

Blooms	Plant Height	Flower sizr	Origin	Life-form
July-Nov	<6.5 ft	Small Clusters	Native	Per

Unlike the Golden Fleece, this prefers damp surroundings and will usually be found alongside water, either streams or ponds. It is a smaller, usually erect plant (<6.5 ft) and has both ray and disk flowers. Its leaves tend to be erect and, while narrow, are not sharp-tipped like those of the Golden Fleece.

California Goldenrod
Solidago velutina ssp. *californica* *

Blooms	Plant Height	Flower size	Origin	Life-form
July-Oct	8-60 in	Large Clusters	Native	Per

Except for the flowers, this is very different from the Western Goldenrod. Found in both sun and shade, the flowers may appear as a tall spike or a loose arch. Each inflorescence has 6-11 ray flowers, usually clustered on one side of the stem. The alternate lanceolate leaves tend to be longer towards the base than the tip of the stem.

Sneezeweed
Helenium puberulum

Blooms	Plant Height	Flower size	Origin	Life-form
June-Aug	20-64 in	Medium	Native	Ann-per

Usually found alongside or near water, this has small spherical heads on very long slender stems. The ray flowers are typically folded back down the stem. The basal and lower cauline leaves are large, oblanceolate and alternate. The common name derives from the use of dried leaves of some Heleniums to make snuff and promote sneezing to rid the body of evil spirits.

Golden Yarrow
Eriophyllum confertiflorum var. *confertiflorum*

Blooms	Plant Height	Flower size	Origin	Life-form
Apr-Aug	8-28 in	Small	Native	Shrub/subshrub

Very common in Garland Ranch, this is a small shrub with bright yellow flower heads at the end of long branching stems. Often confused with Lizard Tail, it can be distinguished, usually, by its smaller leaves and white stems and, with certainty, by the number of its ray flowers; typically 4-5 as compared to the 6-9 of the Lizard Tail.

Lizard Tail
Eriophyllum staechadifolium

Blooms	Plant Height	Flower size	Origin	Life-form
Apr-Sept	12-60 in	Small	Native	Subshrub

Common by the coast, this Yarrow can also be found in Garland Ranch. Its common name derives from its leaves which, upside down, resemble a rather short-tailed lizard. The individual flowers have 6-9 rays (compared to the 4-5 of the Golden Yarrow *(E. confertiflorum)* and it has denser flower heads.

Bristly Ox-tongue
Helminthotheca echioides *

Blooms	Plant Height	Flower size	Origin	Life-form
Apr-Dec	12-30 in	Medium	Eur #	Ann

Definitely not a contender for the most attractive plant in Garland Ranch, this is usually found in waste areas but often near water. It has a number of branches with clusters of Dandelion-like flowers at the tips. The bristly phyllaries, stems and leaves amply justify the plant's common name.

Prickly Lettuce
Lactuca serriola

Blooms	Plant Height	Flower size	Origin	Life-form
June-Oct	20-60 in	Small	Eur	Ann

Despite its appearance, this is the nearest wild relative to the cultivated lettuce. It has many small pale yellow flowers, mostly in open panicle-like clusters. The flowers usually close by midday. Its leaves have spiny edges and are coarsely lobed. The plant is edible though reportedly bitter and it had a variety of interesting uses among ancient and native peoples.

Telegraph Weed
Heterotheca grandiflora

Blooms	Plant Height	Flower size	Origin	Life-form
Jan-Dec	>80 in	Medium	Native	Ann- S/L per

Very common, especially in open areas at the lower levels. Sometimes a very scruffy plant, it is at its best in late summer when it grows into a tall slender plant with numerous inflorescences; each of which has many (30-75) ray flowers and produces a dandelion-like seed head after flowering.

Hairy Golden Aster
Heterotheca sessiliflora ssp. *echioides*

Blooms	Plant Height	Flower size	Origin	Life-form
July-Oct	12-30 in	Medium	Native	Per

Not uncommon in grassland and oak woodlands, this can have a wide range of ray flowers (3-30), 3-10 mm in length. It has noticeably hairy stems and grayish-green leaves. The plant can be very variable in appearance and distinctions between members of the species are subtle.

Smooth Cat's Ear
Hypochaeris glabra

Blooms	Plant Height	Flower size	Origin	Life-form
Mar-Sept	4-16 in	Small	Eur #	Ann-per

This is a common, mildly invasive species, typically found in grassland areas, often in large numbers. It has a rosette of smooth, shallowly lobed, mostly hairless leaves and either a single or a small number of stems with small dandelion-like flowers (i.e. ligules only and no disk flowers). The phyllaries are purple-tipped and (unlike the Common Dandelion) not reflexed.

Hairy Cat's Ear
Hypochaeris radicata

Blooms	Plant Height	Flower size	Origin	Life-form
Apr-Nov	16-30 in	Medium	Eur ##	Ann-per

This is a moderately invasive species. The flowers are very similar to the Smooth Cat's Ear *(H. glabra)* but twice the size and the plant is much larger. The rounded, lobed basal leaves are noticeably hairy. The phyllaries are purple-tipped and not reflexed. Note that the flower has many fewer ligules than the Common Dandelion.

Pineapple Weed
Matricaria discoidea *

Blooms	Plant Height	Flower size	Origin	Life-form
Apr-Aug	4-12 in	Small	NW N America	Ann

This is a common low growing weed with small round heads comprising only disk flowers. When crushed, the flowers give off a pineapple-like aroma. When bruised and rubbed on the skin, the plant is said to provide an effective if temporary insect repellent.

Common Dandelion
Taraxacum officinale

Blooms	Plant Height	Flower size	Origin	Life-form
Jan-Dec	4-16 in	Large	Eur	Per

This is a very common weed found in lawns and waste places. Note the very large number of ligules as compared to the two Cat's Ears (*Hypochaeris glabra & radicata*), and the large, smooth but coarsely-lobed leaves resembling a slightly rounded, barbed arrow head. Note also how the outer phyllaries are 'reflexed' (i.e. curving sharply outwards and downwards).

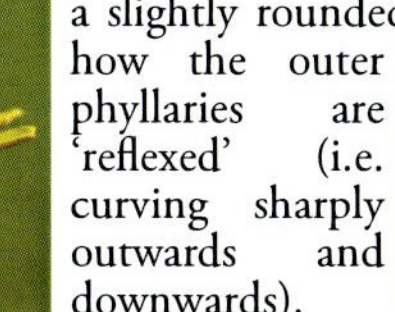

California Goldfields
Lasthenia gracilis

Blooms	Plant Height	Flower size	Origin	Life-form
Mar-May	<16 in	Medium	Native	Ann

Although its flowers are individually attractive, this plant is most noted for its ability to cover entire fields or hillsides with a brilliant gold carpet. The leaves are long and narrow. The flowers are best seen in Garland Ranch in the meadow off East Garzas Road by the trail head that leads to Garzas Creek.

Common Lessingia / Valley Vinegar Weed
Lessingia pectinata var. *tenuipes* *

Blooms	Plant Height	Flower size	Origin	Life-form
May-Nov	2-30 in	Small	Native	Ann

This is common in grassland or scrub areas at the lower levels and can grow in huge numbers. It has no ray flowers but the distinctive funnel-shaped disk flowers all have a noticeable deep maroon base. The stems are tan and the leaves, which tend to dessicate at full flowering time, are up to 3 cm long.

Tall Layia
Layia hieracioides

Blooms	*Plant Height*	*Flower size*	*Origin*	*Life-form*
Apr-May	2-50 in	Small	Native	Ann

This leafy plant is found in shaded woodland areas but it can tolerate open sun. It can be confused with some of the smaller Madias but it can be distinguished with certainty by its rigidly erect, reddish-brown stems covered with black dots and also by its pungent aroma. The 8-16 yellow ray flowers are inconspicuous.

Tidy Tips
Layia platyglossa

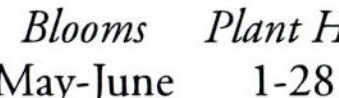

Blooms	*Plant Height*	*Flower size*	*Origin*	*Life-form*
May-June	1-28 in	Medium	Native	Ann

This beautiful flower is unmistakable with its brilliant white-tipped yellow ray flowers. The leaves are slender and lanceolate. The hemispheric phyllaries are characteristic. Tidy Tips can grow in huge numbers, providing spectacular displays (for example in Mark's Ranch). The plant appears to have been recently re-introduced into Garland Ranch.

Common Madia
Madia elegans (includes former ssp. *densifolia)*

A beautiful, extremely common flower of mid to late summer, with a long flowering season. It is very variable, with numerous disk flowers and anything from 5-21 ray flowers, pure yellow in the early season but developing a deep maroon center later on. Often found in profusion with the Lewis' Clarkia. A leafier, taller form was formerly, but is no longer, treated as a separate subspecies.

Slender Tarweed
Madia gracilis

Blooms	*Plant Height*	*Flower size*	*Origin*	*Life-form*
Apr-Aug	4-39 in	Medium	Native	Ann

This is found in shady areas. It lives up to its name with a slender many-branched main stem which produces loose clusters of small flowers which, like other Madias, can be quite variable in appearance. It has 3-10 ray flowers. The leaves are narrow, soft and hairy and the buds are covered in resin glands that give off a tar-like smell.

Coast Tarweed
Madia sativa

Blooms	*Plant Height*	*Flower size*	*Origin*	*Life-form*
May-Oct	14-40 in	Small	Native	Ann

Found in both sun and shade, this plant produces clusters of heads, sometimes a tight cluster at the end of a stem, sometimes more loosely branched. It has 8-13 ray flowers. The flower heads are covered with sticky black glands which give off a strong scent. Both the size of the flower and the plant's growth pattern distinguish it from its namesake, the *Deinandra corymbosa*.

Brewer's Butterweed / Brewer's Senecio
Packera breweri *

Blooms	Plant Height	Flower size	Origin	Life-form
Apr-June	12-30 in	Medium	Native	Per or bienn

Found on wooded or brushy slopes, this produces multiple flowers at the end of its single stem. It has pinnate basal leaves with deeply dissected lobes. Its cauline leaves are also pinnate but much smaller and less dissected.

California Butterweed
Senecio californicus

Blooms	Plant Height	Flower size	Origin	Life-form
Mar-June	4-20 in	Medium	Native	Ann

Found on dry woodland slopes, the flowers are in clusters with 10-15 ray flowers, slightly reflexed (turning down). The anthers may be yellow or black. The long, slender leaves are sometimes serrated and more or less clasping. The receptacle at the top of the stem is naked.

Cut-leaved Fireweed
Senecio glomeratus *

Blooms	Plant Height	Flower size	Origin	Life-form
June-Aug	24-80 in	Small	Australasia	Ann-per

Native to Australia, this is a moderately invasive species. It has multiple heads each with a number of small yellow flat topped flowers. Its long leaves with their many, irregular lobes are distinctive.

Common Groundsel
Senecio vulgaris

Blooms	Plant Height	Flower size	Origin	Life-form
Jan-Dec	4-24 in	Small	Eur, Asia	Ann

Found in open exposed areas. Note black tipped phyllaries with shorter bractlets also black tipped. Cauline leaves are coarsely toothed to pinnate; the clustered basal leaves are broader with no teeth. The branching stems carry loose umbels of bright but inconspicuous yellow disk flowers (55-65 in each head). The green parts of the plant are densely covered in hairs.

Prickly Sow Thistle
Sonchus asper ssp. *asper*

Blooms	Plant Height	Flower size	Origin	Life-form
Jan-Dec	4-55 in	Medium	Eur	Ann

This is slightly less common than the Common Sow Thistle (*S. oleraceus*) but its flower and distinctive bud shape with its broad base and narrow tip are very similar. The leaves, with their teeth and numerous spines are quite different (though still clasping) and, taken with the bud shape, unmistakable.

Common Sow Thistle
Sonchus oleraceus

Blooms	Plant Height	Flower size	Origin	Life-form
Jan-Dec	4-48 in	Medium	Eur	Ann

This is very common and immediately identifiable by its distinctive broad based and strongly tapered bud shape. The leaves are variable in shape, usually finely toothed and sometimes lobed but almost always clasping; i.e. with the base of the leaf surrounding the stem. Some plants exceed 6 ft in height.

Mule Ears
Wyethia glabra

Blooms	Plant Height	Flower size	Origin	Life-form
Mar-May	4-16 in	Large	Native	Per

This is one of the more appropriately named plants with its very large leaves almost overshadowing the striking large flowers. Note the hairless leaves and the rather pointed leaf-like phyllary that may equal or be longer than the ray flowers in this species. There are relatively few specimens in Garland Ranch.

Gray Mule Ears
Wyethia helenioides

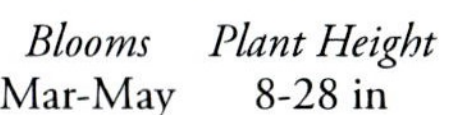

Blooms	Plant Height	Flower size	Origin	Life-form
Mar-May	8-28 in	Large	Native	Per

Similar in appearance and size to the Mule Ears (*W. glabra*), this is distinguished by its larger size but more easily by the felty "tomentose" leaves, i.e. leaves covered with very small hairs. Although this species is unusual in Garland Ranch, another species (*W. mollis*) may be found in huge numbers covering the mountain slopes in parts of the Sierra Nevada.

Blow-Wives
Achyrachaena mollis

Blooms	Plant Height	Flower size	Origin	Life-form
Apr-May	10-16 in	Small	Native	Ann

The fruit of this plant is much more impressive than the inconspicuous yellow ray flowers which turn red (as can be seen in the head visible in the lower half of the large picture). The fruit consist of the 'pappus' (10 shiny white scales in two series) arising from the black body.

Uropappus / Silverpuffs
Uropappus lindleyi

Blooms	Plant Height	Flower size	Origin	Life-form
Apr-June	2-28 in	Medium	Native	Ann

This plant is immediately recognizable by its prominent fruits; heads of delicate fine silvery pappus, each with 5 slender pointed rays. It is commonly seen in grassy areas and beside the trails. Its small yellow flowers are rarely seen and are very similar to Salsify *(Tragopogon dubius)*; they do however have fewer bracts extending beyond the rays and the phyllaries are unequal in length.

California Barberry
Berberis pinnata ssp. *pinnata*

Blooms	Plant Height	Flower size	Origin	Life-form
Mar-May	16-80 in	Med Cluster	Native	Per / Shrub

This shrub has dark green leaves that closely resemble holly but are not quite as prickly. It has clusters of small yellow flowers which turn into purple fruits. These are said to be edible but not with pleasure. This species can be very difficult to distinguish from the Oregon Grape (*B. aquifolium* var. *dictyota)* with which it intergrades.

Common Fiddleneck
Amsinckia intermedia *

Blooms	Plant Height	Flower size	Origin	Life-form
Apr-Aug	8-48 in	Med Clusters	Native	Ann

This grows in great profusion in open grassland, creating a striking display with its golden flowers and the curved heads which give the plant its name. Note its many tubular yellow flowers with orange spots at the base of the petals. The seeds and foliage are said to be poisonous to cattle.

Whispering Bells
Emmenanthe penduliflora var. *penduliflora*

Blooms	Plant Height	Flower size	Origin	Life-form
Apr-July	4-20 in	Small	Native	Ann

Extremely rare in Garland Ranch, this is a fire follower which may also be found in recently disturbed land. It has a loose growth habit. It has simple leaves, toothed to pinnately lobes and clusters of pale lemon, bell-shaped flowers that may be erect to start with but then droop on their slender stems to justify the plant's scientific name.

American Winter Cress
Barbarea orthoceras

Blooms	Plant Height	Flower size	Origin	Life-form
Mar-July	8-24 in	Small	Native	Bienn

At first sight, this looks like a mustard, but the complete absence of hairs from the leaves and the pinnately lobed leaves that are found just below the flower heads are distinctive. The vivid green coloring is also distinctive.

Charlock Mustard
Sinapis arvensis

Blooms	Plant Height	Flower size	Origin	Life-form
Mar-Oct	12-16 in	Small	Eurasia #	Ann

Not commonly found in Garland Ranch, this is a hairy, leafy plant with elongated clusters of yellow flowers at the end of almost leafless branches. The toothed oval or lobed leaves are largest at the base of the plant. The four-petalled flowers are similar to those of the other mustards.

Black Mustard
Brassica nigra

Blooms	Plant Height	Flower size	Origin	Life-form
Feb-July	1-8 ft	Small	Eur ##	Ann-bienn

This is an untidy looking plant, very common in Garland Ranch. The inflorescence of the Black Mustard is smaller and less bright than that of the Field Mustard *(B. rapa)*. The leaves are very variable, the basal leaves being coarse and pinnately lobed, the cauline leavers being smaller and more or less sessile.

Field Mustard
Brassica rapa

Blooms	Plant Height	Flower size	Origin	Life-form
Jan-June	1-4 ft	Small	Eur #	Ann-bienn

This is a smaller plant than the Black Mustard and can be distinguished by its brighter inflorescence and its more or less clasping and hairless leaves towards the upper part of the stems. Less common than the Black Mustard (*B. nigra*) in Garland Ranch but seen in huge quantities by the roadside and fields.

Hedge Mustard & Tumble Mustard
Sisymbrium officinale & Sisymbrium altissimum

Blooms	Plant Height	Flower size	Origin	Life-form
Apr-Sept	10-30 in	Small	Eur	Ann

These are two less common mustards, distinguishable by their very different leaves. The Tumble Mustard (above and R) has slender pinnately-lobed leaves with the upper leaves being linear to thread like. The Hedge Mustard (L) has one pair of pinnate lobes at the base of each leaf, each lobe normally pointing backwards to form an arrow shape

Douglas' Wallflower / Western Wallflower
Erysimum capitatum ssp. *capitatum*

Blooms	Plant Height	Flower size	Origin	Life-form
May-July	<39 in	Large Clusters	Native	Bienn - per

Although not an uncommon plant, there seem to be comparatively few specimens in Garland Ranch. Its flowers show that it is in the same family as the mustards, but its deeper coloring, ranging from pale to dark orange (with other colors also found in other areas) is very distinctive. It likes hillsides in sun or part shade. Note the long, very slender leaves and thick stem.

Rushrose
Helianthemum scoparium

Blooms	Plant Height	Flower size	Origin	Life-form
Apr-Aug	5-18 in	Small	Native	Per - Subshrub

This is found at higher elevations in dry sandy areas. It forms low, spreading and somewhat matted plants with many beautiful small pale yellow flowers. The stems are slender and almost rush-like but they also bear small linear to narrow lanceolate leaves.

Lance-leaved Dudleya
Dudleya lanceolata

Blooms	Plant Height	Flower size	Origin	Life-form
June-Aug	6-18 in	Small	Native	Per

One of comparatively few succulents to be found in Garland Ranch, this, as the Stonecrop family name suggests, is to be found growing out of rocks. It has long lanceolate basal leaves and a tall stem which bears a number of small reddish-orange flowers which never open more than part way.

Pacific Stonecrop / Broad-leaved Stonecrop
Sedum spathulifolium

Blooms	Plant Height	Flower size	Origin	Life-form
June-July	2-9 in	Small	Native	Per

This is a low growing succulent to be found growing out of rocks in damp, shady areas. Its flowers are an undistinguished greenish yellow star; its rounded basal leaves are more distinctive.

Deerweed
Acmispon glaber var. *glaber* *

Blooms	Plant Height	Flower size	Origin	Life-form
Mar-Aug	20-80 in	Small	Native	Per - Subshrub

A very common shrub found in chaparral and scrub areas, this has numerous long stout stems, both erect and branching, with clusters of 2-7 small yellow flowers arranged in umbels which turn reddish with age. The heads of the flowers are sessile. The fruit is in the form of a curved pod with just 2 seeds.

Coastal Lotus
Acmispson maritimus var. *maritimus* *

Blooms	Plant Height	Flower size	Origin	Life-form
Mar-June	2-6 in	Small	Native	Ann

More common closer to the coast, this Lotus has 1-5 flowers. Note the 'hooked beak' (a result of a keel that is longer than the wings) and the stalk of the flower that is longer than 5 mm which differentiates it from the Chile Lotus (*A. wrangelianus*). There are 5-8 leaflets covered with soft fine hairs.

Bishop's Lotus
Acmispon strigosus *

Blooms	Plant Height	Flower size	Origin	Life-form
Feb-July	2-6 in	Small	Native	Ann

Fairly common in open sunny areas, this has slender, stiff-haired leaves and yellow flowers with red veins. The flowers turn reddish with age. The fruit is a red pod up to 1.25 inches long. Easily confused with the Chile Lotus *(A. wrangelianus)*, but the shape of the 6-10 leaflets is quite distinct.

Chile Lotus / California Lotus
Acmispon wrangelianus *

Blooms	Plant Height	Flower size	Origin	Life-form
Mar-June	2-6 in	Small	Native	Ann

Easily confused with the Bishop's Lotus *(A. strigosus)*, this can be distinguished by its 3-5 broader and more pointed leaflets with fine hairs only around the edges. The flowers are solitary and remain pure yellow. Flowers are more or less sessile, unlike the Bishop's Lotus.

Large-flowered Lotus / Chaparral Lotus
Acmispon grandiflorus *

Blooms	Plant Height	Flower size	Origin	Life-form
Apr-June	2-6 in	Medium	Native	Per

Fairly uncommon in Garland Ranch, this has unmistakable flowers ranging from creamy-yellow to a deep pinkish-red. Each stem has 7-9 pointed oval leaflets. The seed pod can be up to 2.5 inches long.

Bird's-Foot Trefoil
Lotus corniculatus

Blooms	Plant Height	Flower size	Origin	Life-form
June-Sept	2-6 in	Small	Eurasia	Per

Commonly found in grassland in mid to late summer, this has umbels of 3-6 bright yellow flowers often with red veins and sometimes with a reddish tinge. The slender and pointed leaflets are in groups of 5 but with the central 3 raised above the others and being most prominent.

French Broom
Genista monspessulana

Blooms	Plant Height	Flower size	Origin	Life-form
Mar-May	<10 ft	Medium	Medit ###	Shrub

Certainly one of the most aggressively invasive shrubs to be found in Garland Ranch, this has small oval evergreen leaves and a profusion of bright yellow flowers. The mature seed pods burst open with force spreading the seeds over a wide area. One mature plant can produce 100,000 seeds in a season.

Spanish Broom
Spartium junceum

Blooms	Plant Height	Flower size	Origin	Life-form
Mar-June	<10 ft	Medium	Medit ###	Shrub

Although regarded as highly invasive, this is not common in Garland Ranch. Unlike the French Broom *(Genista monspessulana)* its rush-like stems bear only a few deciduous leaves. Its flowers are a little larger, paler and more delicate than those of the French Broom.

Bur Clover
Medicago polymorpha

Blooms	Plant Height	Flower size	Origin	Life-form
Mar-June	4-16 in	Small	Medit #	Ann

This invasive species has small pure yellow flowers and roundish sometimes almost heart shaped leaves. It produces small burs. A related, but less invasive species, the Spotted Bur Clover *(M. arabica)* (lower R), is similar but for the dark blotch in the center of the leaves.

Indian Melilot & White Sweet Clover
Melilotus indicus & Melilotus albus

Blooms	Plant Height	Flower size	Origin	Life-form
Apr-Oct	4-24 in	Med Cluster	Medit / Eurasia	Ann-bien

A tallish plant, Indian Melilot has slender slightly toothed leaves and dense clusters of small tubular yellow flowers. Sometimes known as Sweet Clover or Sour Clover, it has been used as a source of nectar for bees and also as a forage crop. A white version *(M. albus)* is also found; this can be a substantially larger plant, up to 6 ft in height. Both flowers and leaves are fragrant.

Shamrock / Little Hop Clover & Hop Clover
Trifolium dubium & Trifolium campestre

Blooms	Plant Height	Flower size	Origin	Life-form
May-July	8-16 in	Small	Eur	Ann

Fairly common in grassland, this has distinctive heads with 5-10 flowers arranged in umbels. The leaves are oval and finely toothed. The Hop Clover *(T. campestre)* (Below M & R) is similar but has larger heads with, usually, 20 flowers. Its banner has noticeable veins. Neither has an involucre.

Fremontia / Flannel Bush
Fremontodendron californicum

Blooms	Plant Height	Flower size	Origin	Life-form
Apr-May	10-18 ft	Large	Native	Shrub / Sm Tree

This large shrub or small tree is commonly seen in freeway dividers and to be found by the main parking area for Garland Ranch. It has a profusion of large yellow flowers. Its leaves are leathery and covered with coarse hairs that make handling them without gloves a painful proposition.

Yellow Mariposa Lily
Calochortus luteus

Blooms	Plant Height	Flower size	Origin	Life-form
Blooms	*Plant Height*	*Flower size*	*Origin*	*Life-form*
May-June	8-20 in	Large	Native	Bulb

This spectacular tulip-shaped flower is found in open grassland, sometimes in considerable numbers. It is attractive to butterflies (such as this Chalcedon Checkerspot). It has even more spectacular relatives, some of them found in the Pinnacles. Like all members of this genus, petals and sepals are in 3's.

Leopard Lily
Lilium pardalinum ssp. *pardalinum*

Blooms	Plant Height	Flower size	Origin	Life-form
Blooms	*Plant Height*	*Flower size*	*Origin*	*Life-form*
June-July	4-8 ft	Large	Native	Bulb

This beautiful lily is to be found alongside streams, most accessibly in Kahn Ranch. Each plant has multiple flowers and it is without question the most spectacular flower to be found in Garland Ranch. In some parts of the world, this is called a Turk's Cap Lily because of the shape formed by the upturned petals.

Contorted primrose
Camissonia contorta

Blooms	Plant Height	Flower size	Origin	Life-form
Mar-June	<12 in	Small	Native	Ann

This small primrose is found in open grassland. It has bright yellow flowers with a small red blotch at the base of the petals. Its leaves are narrow and pointed with dentate margins. Its most distinctive feature is the extraordinary contorted shape of the seed pods.

Small Primrose
Camissoniopsis micrantha *

Blooms	Plant Height	Flower size	Origin	Life-form
Mar-May	0-24 in	Very Small	Native	Ann

The flowers are very similar to the Contorted Primrose *(Camissonia contorta)*, but somewhat smaller (approx 5 mm across). The leaves are broader than the Contorted Primrose and the plant is covered with long soft hairs.

Suncups
Taraxia ovata *

Bermuda Buttercup
Oxalis pes-caprae

Blooms	Plant Height	Flower size	Origin	Life-form
Mar-June	0-4 in	Medium	Native	Per

Blooms	Plant Height	Flower size	Origin	Life-form
Nov-Mar	6-12 in	Medium	S Africa ##	Ann

This very low growing plant is common in the early to mid-spring. It has a dense basal rosette of oval to lanceolate, sometimes wavy, leaves. Its 4-petalled flowers are a brilliant lemon yellow.

Although invasive, this Oxalis is attractive with its profusion of bright yellow flowers that appear by roadsides and in disturbed areas in the winter and continue through the early spring. The flowers close up in the evening. Once established, it is very difficult to eradicate since it propagates itself through small bulblets.

Yellow Sorrel & Dwarf & Hairy Wood Sorrels
Oxalis corniculata & *O. micrantha* * & *O. pilosa* *

Blooms	Plant Height	Flower size	Origin	Life-form
Jan-Dec	<12 in	Small	Eur-Medit	Per

These three sorrels have very similar flowers; the alien Yellow Sorrel (Top) being distinguished by small red dots at the base of the petals. Of the two native Wood Sorrels, the Dwarf Wood Sorrel *(O. micrantha)* (L) is shorter but has longer flower stems and more flowers on each stem (6-14); the Hairy Wood Sorrel *(O. pilosa)* (R) is taller and has 1-3 flowers.

Narrow-leaved Meconella
Hesperomecon linearis *

Blooms	Plant Height	Flower size	Origin	Life-form
Mar-June	2-10 in	Medium	Native	Ann

Not uncommon in open grassy areas or trailsides, this plant is distinctive with its alternating and overlapping white and yellow or yellow edged petals. It is easy to confuse with Cream Cups *(Platystemon californicus)* but its coloration is more marked and the partially open flowers do not have the bowl shape of the Cream Cups. Note the hairy stems.

California Poppy
Eschscholzia californica var. *californica*

Blooms	*Plant Height*	*Flower size*	*Origin*	*Life-form*
Feb-Sept	2-24 in	Large	Native	Ann-per

The state flower of California, this needs no introduction. With its simple elegant shape and its vivid orange (and/or yellow) color, it is immediately recognizable. Note the spreading green or pinkish disk-like receptacle at the base of the flower which distinguishes it from the Tufted Poppy.

Tufted Poppy
Eschscholzia caespitosa

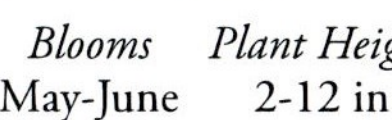

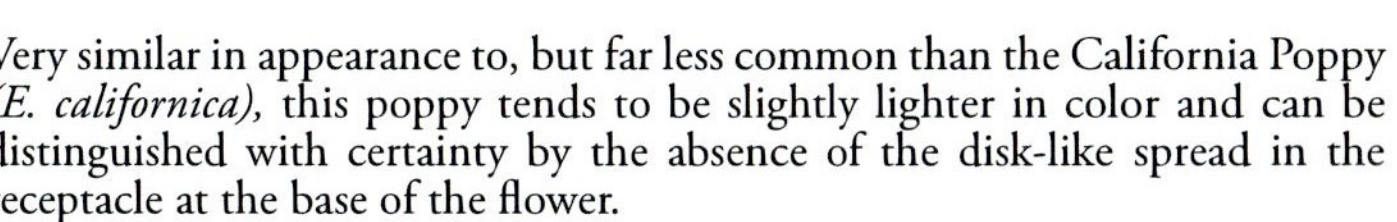

Blooms	*Plant Height*	*Flower size*	*Origin*	*Life-form*
May-June	2-12 in	Large	Native	Ann-per

Very similar in appearance to, but far less common than the California Poppy (*E. californica*), this poppy tends to be slightly lighter in color and can be distinguished with certainty by the absence of the disk-like spread in the receptacle at the base of the flower.

Sticky Monkey Flower
Mimulus aurantiacus var. *aurantiacus*

Blooms	Plant Height	Flower size	Origin	Life-form
Mar-Aug	4-60 in	Medium	Native	Subshrub/shrub

A very common shrub, this is immediately recognizable with its bright orange tubular flowers, almost always arranged in pairs. The narrow lanceolate leaves are opposite and appear all the way up the stem. They are distinctly sticky to the touch. The 2-lobed white stigmas of the flower will close if touched or if they receive pollen.

Santa Lucia Sticky Monkey Flower
Mimulus aurantiacus var. *grandiflorus* *

Blooms	Plant Height	Flower size	Origin	Life-form
Apr-July	4-60 in	Medium	Native	Subshrub/shrub

This is an uncommon variety of the Sticky Monkey Flower (*M. aurantiacus* var. *a.*) and only a few specimens are known in Garland Ranch although it is common at higher elevations in the Santa Lucia mountains. Its flowers are larger, variable in color, typically (though not always) shading from pale orange to white and its notched lobes are distinctive.

Common Monkey Flower / Seep Monkey Flower
Mimulus guttatus

Blooms	Plant Height	Flower size	Origin	Life-form
Mar-Aug	8-60 in	Medium	Native	Ann-per / Rhiz.

This plant is to be found in only a few places in Garland Ranch, in damp locations, by stream beds or on the face of waterfalls. Its bright yellow flowers are unmistakable and the bladder-like seed pods are also very distinctive. The maroon spots on the petals are distinctive in this species. Roots develop where the stems touch the ground.

Golden Brodiaea / Pretty Face
Triteleia ixioides ssp. *ixioides*

Blooms	Plant Height	Flower size	Origin	Life-form
May-Aug	8-30 in	Medium	Native	Per - Corm

This beautiful flower is very common in late spring to mid summer. Found in grassland and along the edges of trails, it has a single stem with multiple golden yellow star shaped flowers with brown central veins - amply justifying its common name.

Prickle-fruited Buttercup
Ranunculus muricatus

Blooms	Plant Height	Flower size	Origin	Life-form
Apr-June	6-20 in	Medium	Eurasia	Ann-bienn

Comparatively unusual and usually found in damp or heavily shaded areas, this plant is very different from the California Buttercup *(R. californicus)* with its five separated petals and its often rounded, deeply lobed yellowish-green leaves. Its fruit has small spines which give the plant its common name.

California Buttercup & Downy Buttercup
Ranunculus californicus var. *c & R. hebecarpus*

Blooms	Plant Height	Flower size	Origin	Life-form
Feb-May	7-28 in	Medium	Native	Per

This plant is extremely common in both sun and shade. It is quite variable in appearance with between 5 and 27 shiny petals. The leaves are also variable from narrow and lanceolate to 3-lobed dissected wedges at the base. The uncommon Downy Buttercup (below R) is small and delicate with the 5 hooked, disk-like fruits (2-3 mm across) more apparent than the tiny flowers.

Johnny Jump-Up
Viola pedunculata

Blooms	Plant Height	Flower size	Origin	Life-form
Feb-May	2-15 in	Medium	Native	Per

This delightful small pansy is very commonly found in open grassland in the early spring. There is no mistaking its happy yellow face with dark brown veining. The leaves are variable, including both heart-shaped and spade-shaped forms. Also known as 'wild pansy'.

Puncture-vine
Tribulus terrestris

Blooms	Plant Height	Flower size	Origin	Life-form
Apr-Oct	<6 in	Small	Medit	Ann

Found in numbers in the meadow off East Garzas, this has opposite, bright green leaflets and bright yellow flowers borne in the axils of the leaves. The fruit consist of 4-5 spiny burs which damage animals and bicycle tires. Tribulus means a 3-pointed caltrop, an ancient weapon still in use today.

California Sagebrush / Coast Sagebrush
Artemisia californica

Blooms	Plant Height	Flower size	Origin	Life-form
Aug-Dec	2-5 ft	Small	Native	Shrub

This small aromatic shrub is common in Garland Ranch and even more so by the coast, preferring dry sunny positions. It has dense feathery bluish-green foliage and produces small reddish pendulous flowers in late summer and fall. The leaves can be used in cooking although the plant is not a true sage.

Lamb's Quarters
Chenopodium album

Blooms	Plant Height	Flower size	Origin	Life-form
June-Oct	8-40 in	Small	Eur	Ann

At first sight this might be mistaken for Mugwort or a Dock but the tight powdery clusters of flowers/fruits (typical of several Goosefoots) with tiny 5-pointed greenish-yellow flowers are distinctive. The leaves (15-70 mm long) are dull green above, lanceolate and slightly dentate. The plant is cultivated as a food crop in some parts of the world, especially North India.

Pitseed Goosefoot & Narrow-leaved Goosefoot
Chenopodium berlandieri & Chenopodium pratericola

Blooms	Plant Height	Flower size	Origin	Life-form
Jun-Oct	12-24 in	Small	Native	Ann

These two Goosefoots have a similar bushy appearance. The Pitseed Goosefoot (above and L) is sometimes mistaken for Lamb's Quarters *(C. album),* but its seeds have (under magnification) a honeycomb-pitted appearance and its leaves are smaller (15-30 mm) and slightly translucent. The Narrow-leaved Goosefoot (R) has longer, more slender leaves and minutely wrinkled seeds.

California Goosefoot & Nettle-leaved Goosefoot
Chenopodium californicum & Chenopodium murale

Blooms	Plant Height	Flower size	Origin	Life-form
Mar-June	8-36 in	Small	Native	Per

California Goosefoot is not common in Garland Ranch but is easily recognized by its large (4-10 cm) coarsely-toothed leaves and long spike of flowers and fruits. The European native Nettle-leaved Goosefoot (R) is a smaller plant with much smaller (0.8-4 cm) toothed ovate to deltate leaves and numerous clusters of flowers and fruits growing along and at the tips of the stems.

Durango root
Datisca glomerata

Blooms	Plant Height	Flower size	Origin	Life-form
May-July	2-6 ft	Small	Native	Per

Commonly found in or by stream beds, this resembles a tall nettle with its long, slender, sharply toothed leaves. It has many small flowers with multiple filaments but no petals. It belongs to a rare group of plants that are androdioecious, i.e. having male and hermaphrodite but no female members. All parts of the plant are toxic.

Hoary Nettle and Dwarf Nettle
Urtica dioica ssp. *holosericea* & *Urtica urens*

Blooms	Plant Height	Flower size	Origin	Life-form
June-Sept	3-10 ft	Med clusters	Native	Per

Both of these nettles are common, usually found in woodland or moist areas. The Hoary Nettle has large (6-20 cm) coarsely serrated leaves, gray-hairy on the underside, and often drooping clusters of small flowers. The European native Dwarf Nettle is an annual. It is a much smaller plant (>2 ft tall) with smaller (2-4 cm), slightly broader leaves and clusters of flowers growing along but close to the stem. Both plants can deliver an unpleasant sting.

Petty Spurge
Euphorbia peplus

Blooms	Plant Height	Flower size	Origin	Life-form
Feb-Aug	4-18 in	Small	Eur	Ann

Note the horned nectar glands of the flower and the red stems. For years people in Australia have cured certain cancerous spots on the skin by applying the fresh milky sap from *E. peplus* directly to the lesions. This (patented) process is said to produce essentially the same result as when a dermatologist applies liquid nitrogen directly to a superficial cancerous growth on the skin.

Checker Lily / Mission Bells
Fritillaria affinis

Blooms	Plant Height	Flower size	Origin	Life-form
Feb-Mar	4-48 in	Large	Native	Bulb

This beautiful lily typically appears in early spring, preferring full or partial shade. Individual flowers (comparatively small for a lily, 1-4 cm long) are very short-lived. Its petals are yellowish-green with purple mottling although the species is highly variable in appearance.

Giant Trillium
Trillium chloropetalum

Blooms	Plant Height	Flower size	Origin	Life-form
Jan-Apr	8-28 in	Large	Native	Rhizome

Three large green leaves grow whorled around the stout unbranched stem just below the single 3-petalled flower. The flower arises directly from the center of the leaves. Neither leaves nor flowers have stems. The petals and sepals are erect and vary from maroon to purple in color. Found in shady woodlands, it appears to thrive on damp conditions.

Helleborine
Epipactis helleborine

Blooms	Plant Height	Flower size	Origin	Life-form
July-Aug	16-39 in	Small	Eur	Per

Many specimens of this orchid can be found along both sides of the Carmel River. Its long lanceolate leaves are typical of the orchid family and its slender drooping stem (before flowering) is characteristic. The flowers are green with a pale purplish tinge and a very dark, almost black throat. Sometimes confusingly called "Hellebore", but unrelated to the *Helleborus* genus.

Bird's beak
Cordylanthus rigidus ssp. *rigidus*

Blooms	*Plant Height*	*Flower size*	*Origin*	*Life-form*
Aug-Sept	12-60 in	Small	Native	Ann

This can be found in large numbers on either side of the trail on the steep eastern end of Snively's Ridge. It has a loose, much-branched appearance with linear leaves. Its small white flowers are shaped like a bird's beak with a U-shaped maroon stripe and are surrounded by leaf-like bracts which are lobed in their lower half.

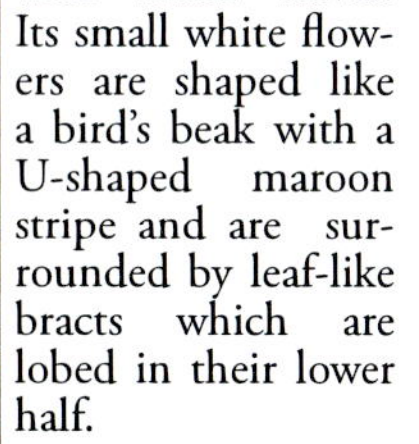

Clustered Dock / Green Dock
Rumex conglomeratus

Blooms	*Plant Height*	*Flower size*	*Origin*	*Life-form*
Mar-Oct	<60 in	Small	Eur	Per

This very common dock has long slender leaves, getting smaller as they ascend the stem. The flowers and seeds are clustered in small groups up the stem, in marked distinction to the Curly Dock (*R. crispus*) and Fiddle Dock (*R. pulcher*). 'Callosities' (small whitish lumps) are present on all valves and are wider than the valves. The callosities and valves vary among the species.

Curly Dock
Rumex crispus

Blooms	*Plant Height*	*Flower size*	*Origin*	*Life-form*
Apr-Aug	<60 in	Very Small	Eurasia #	Per

This species of Dock is common and invasive. The inconspicuous small green flowers ripen into winged seeds. The eye-catching seed heads of Docks are of interest because of the great variation from one species to another of the valves and callosities and the teeth present on the margin of the valves in some species (see p. 184). This dock is a useful antidote to Stinging Nettle.

Fiddle Dock
Rumex pulcher

Blooms	*Plant Height*	*Flower size*	*Origin*	*Life-form*
May-Sept	0-39 in	Very Small	Medit	Per

This is another common Dock. Unlike some of the other Docks, this has callosities on each of its valves. It also has teeth (5-10) on each margin of the valves (compared to 3-5 for the Bitter Dock *(R. obtusifolius)*). The branches often grow at right angles from the main stem. The imaginatively-minded may see a fiddle shape in some of its leaves.

Fendler's Meadow-Rue
Thalictrum fendleri var. *fendleri*

Blooms	Plant Height	Flower size	Origin	Life-form
Apr-July	24-80 in	Medium	Native	Per

Although not uncommon, it is easy to miss this fairly inconspicuous plant. It is dioecious, with male and female flowers normally borne on separate plants. Its small male flowers are quite striking with their dangling greenish-purple bell-shaped inflorescence and multiple stamens with large anthers. The female flowers are a cluster of immature fruits tipped with pink styles.

Burnet / Small (or Garden) Burnet
Poterium sanguisorba *

Blooms	Plant Height	Flower size	Origin	Life-form
May-June	8-20 in	Small	Eur	Per

Very commonly found in open grassland, the tight head of this plant produces very small red flowers and long thread-like stamens and pistils. The oval leaves are much toothed and can (as the name suggests) be used in salads. It used to be popular and was brought to the USA by early English settlers.

Fern-like Azolla & Long-leaved Pondweed
Azolla filiculoides & Potamogeton nodosus

These two plants are found on Veeder Pond. The Azolla can blanket the pond in late spring turning the whole pond red. In some parts of the world it has been grown for its nitrogen-fixing ability so enhancing the growth rate of crops like rice. The Long-leaved Pondweed (lower R) appears later in the summer and has distinctive elliptic-lanceolate leaves with parallel veins. Note the small flower spike. The Pondweed is a perennial, growing from submerged rhizomes.

Tall Cyperus
Cyperus eragrostis

Blooms	*Plant Height*	*Flower size*	*Origin*	*Life-form*
May-Nov	8-30 in	Med Clusters	Native	Per

This is a very common small sedge, with long narrow rays (distinct from the leaves nearer the base of the plant), projecting from the flower head at the tip of the stem. Note the mass of flat, toothed fruits at the base of the rays.

California Tule
Schoenoplectus californicus *

Blooms	Plant Height	Flower size	Origin	Life-form
May-Aug	<15 ft	Large clusters	Native	Per

Commonly found in ponds and streams, this large sedge, with its rounded, triangular stems, is best known for its many uses by indigenous peoples. These included building houses ("ruks"), boats or canoes. Closer to the shoreline, it plays an important role as a buffer against wind and tides, preventing erosion and allowing more sensitive plants to become established.

Panicled Bulrush
Scirpus microcarpus

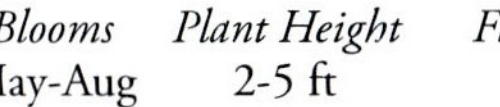

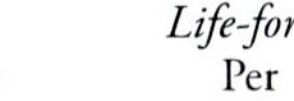

Blooms	Plant Height	Flower size	Origin	Life-form
May-Aug	2-5 ft	Small	Native	Per

This sedge (not a rush, despite its name) is not uncommon, found alongside streams. It produces a spreading panicle of small white flowers. Note the triangular upper stem - characteristic of sedges. This tallies with the popular saying 'Reeds and rushes are round but sedges have edges'.

Braun's Scouring Rush & Giant Horsetail
Equisetum laevigatum & *Equisetum telmateia* ssp. *braunii*

These two are among the five members to be found in California of one of oldest plant families. It is said that for over 100 million years, members of this family (then far more diverse, some forming trees 30 meters tall) dominated the woodlands of the Palaeozoic period (roughly 540-250 million years ago). The scouring rush (R) is so called because its stems are coated in abrasive silicates which made it useful for scouring utensils. The same is true of the Horsetail (L). The common name of the Horsetail needs no explanation.

Narrow-leaved Cat-tail & Broad-leaved Cat-tail
Typha angustifolia & *Typha latifolia*

Blooms	Plant Height	Flower size	Origin	Life-form
June-July	3-9 ft	Large	Native	Per

Cat-tails are easily identified by their dense but soft flowering heads and their crescent shaped leaves (in cross-section). Identifying the species is far more difficult since their size and appearance can overlap and the species readily hybridise. The form found at Garland Ranch (R) is slightly larger than the typical *T. angustifolia* but much smaller than the typical *T. latifolia* (upper L).

Brown-Headed Rush & Common Wood Rush
Juncus phaeocephalus var. *phaeocephalus* & *Luzula comosa* var. *c*

Spreading Rush
Juncus patens

Blooms	Plant Height	Flower size	Origin	Life-form
May-June	4-20 in	Medium	Native	Per

These are two fairly common rushes found in shady or grassy areas; they do not form dense plants like the Spreading Rush (*Juncus patens*). The flowers appear terminal (at the end of the stems). Note the long pink anthers of the Brown-headed Rush (L) as compared to the yellow anther filaments of the Common Wood Rush (R).

Blooms	Plant Height	Flower size	Origin	Life-form
June-July	16-30 in	Medium	Native	Per

A very common rush, found in moist places, this has bluish-green stems which are abruptly sharp-pointed (i.e. they taper only very close to the tip). Note how the flowers appear laterally off the stem, initially close to it but then arching outwards.

Chain Fern
Woodwardia fimbriata

The largest of the ferns to be found in Garland Ranch, this likes damp conditions and is found in or by stream beds. The individual leaves are clearly separated and the segments are each pointed and very finely serrated. The common name derives from the neat lines created by the oblong 'sori' (containing the spores) which are visible on both the surface and underside of each leaflet.

Sword Fern
Polystichum munitum

This is comparatively uncommon in Garland Ranch although it is one of the most commonly found ferns elsewhere, especially in Redwood forests. Its leaves are more slender than those of the Wood Fern, even more sharply pointed and the individual finely serrated leaflets are not segmented. The broadened base of each leaflet is said to resemble the hilt of a sword. Like the Wood Fern, this is to be found throughout the year.

Wood Fern
Dryopteris arguta

Perhaps the most common fern in Garland Ranch, this is to be found throughout the year on shaded hillsides. Although the bipinnate leaves are lanceolate, the individual segments tend to be rounded and often finely toothed. Note the rounded sori.

Western Bracken Fern
Pteridium aquilinum var. *pubescens*

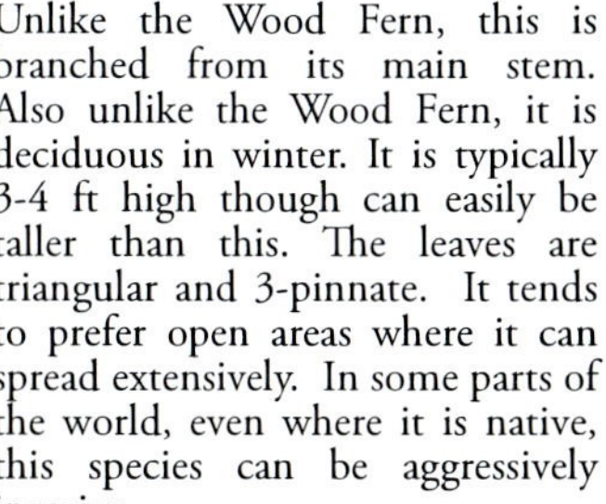

Unlike the Wood Fern, this is branched from its main stem. Also unlike the Wood Fern, it is deciduous in winter. It is typically 3-4 ft high though can easily be taller than this. The leaves are triangular and 3-pinnate. It tends to prefer open areas where it can spread extensively. In some parts of the world, even where it is native, this species can be aggressively invasive.

California Polypody
Polypodium californicum

This is a very common fern, appearing in shaded woodland areas, often on rocky ledges, soon after the first seasonal rains and dying back during the course of the summer. Note the rounded ends of each leaf and the twin rows of round sori on the underside of each leaf.

Licorice Fern
Polypodium glycyrrhiza

Very similar to the California Polypody, this has tapered, pointed leaves. It has been known to hybridize with the California Polypody. Its name derives from the licorice flavour of the rhizome.

Five-finger Fern
Adiantum aleuticum

So far as is known, this is found in only one place in Garland Ranch, on the face of the Waterfall on the Waterfall trail. It is a particularly beautiful fern, with the same black stems as the Maidenhair Fern and drooping fronds with delicate leaflets fringed on the lower rim.

California Maidenhair Fern & Venus-hair Fern
Adiantum jordanii & Adiantum capillus-veneris

This is a very common but beautifully delicate fern which appears shortly after the first rains and dies back during the the summer. It has fine black stems and fan shaped leaves which may be slightly lobed (<1/4 way to the base). The much less common Venus-hair Fern (below L) is similar but has larger, distinctly-lobed (cut >1/4 way to the base) leaves on drooping fronds.

Coffee Fern & Bird's-foot Fern
Pellaea andromedifolia & Pellaea mucronata

The Coffee Fern has small (6-15 mm) rounded-oval leaves which are notice-ably tougher than most ferns and a unique shade of green. This and its low spreading growth pattern make it easy to mistake for a small shrub. The very uncommon Bird's-foot Fern is similar but with smaller (2-6 mm), narrow, oblong leaves which are "mucronate", i.e. they have a small point at the tip.

Goldback Fern
Pentagramma triangularis ssp. *triangularis*

This is a small fern, looking slightly like a small Wood Fern, but distinguish-able by its two backward pointing leaves at the base of the frond and black stems. The underside of the leaves is greenish-gold in color and covered in a powdery exudate. If pressed against skin or clothing, this leave a clear impression which gives the plant its other common name, 'the Tattoo Fern'. The leaves die back in the late summer and form beautiful golden curls.

Round Woolly Marbles & Slender Woolly-heads
*Psilocarphus chilensis * & Psilocarphus tenellus*

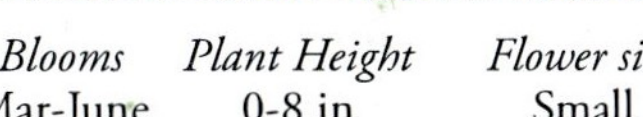

Blooms	Plant Height	Flower size	Origin	Life-form
Mar-June	0-8 in	Small	Native	Ann

This uncommon plant is found mostly in hard-packed soil or sometimes in dry mud or vernal pools. It is gray-green in color, prostrate and branching and loosely woolly. There are only disk flowers. The oval leaves are appressed to the flower head. Slender Woolly-heads (lower R) is similar but its leaves are more slender and spreading. It also likes hard-packed soil.

Wayside Pepper Grass
Lepidium strictum

Blooms	Plant Height	Flower size	Origin	Life-form
Mar-May	1-2 in	Very Small	Native	Ann

This is a diminutive, prostrate relative of the Common Pepper Grass. Its fruits are very similar to those of its larger relative but about half the size (2.5 - 3.5mm). It is common along trails in open sunny positions and may be found growing with or even in Sand Mat.

Sand Mat
Cardionema ramosissimum

Blooms	Plant Height	Flower size	Origin	Life-form
Apr-Aug	<1.5 in	Very snall	Native	Per

Very common along trails in sunny positions, this forms a prostrate mat of gray-green foliage which has minute greenish flowers surrounded by fine white hairs. These are barely visible without a hand lens. The foliage is surprisingly prickly.

Moss Pygmyweed & Sand Pygmy
Crassula tillaea & Crassula connata

Sand Pygmy

Blooms	Plant Height	Flower size	Origin	Life-form
Feb-May	1-2 in	Very small	Medit	Ann

These are very small erect plants growing in open dry areas. Moss Pygmyweed is non-native and has 2 tiny (1-1.5 mm) flowers per leaf; the leaves being very small (1-3 mm) and oval to oblong. The plants turns reddish with age. There is a very similar (native) Sand Pygmy (*C. connata*) which has 4 erect sepals rather than 3 outcurved ones; this is much less common at Garland Ranch.

Dwarf Owl's Clover
Triphysaria pusilla

Blooms	Plant Height	Flower size	Origin	Life-form
Apr-May	< 1in	Very small	Native	Ann

This can be as much as 8 in high though is typically much smaller. The foliage is green and then turns reddish-brown. The tiny flowers, appearing in April-May, are almost invisible to the naked eye but, under a hand lens, show themselves to be a pouch, dark red on top and with the lower lips also dark red.

Common Knotweed
Polygonum aviculare ssp. *depressum* *

Blooms	Plant Height	Flower size	Origin	Life-form
Mar-Nov	<6 in	Very Small	Worldwide	Ann

A common noxious weed, this survives drought conditions and thrives on compacted soils (such as trails). The plant is often, though not always prostrate, forming small mats. The flowers are tiny (3-5 mm across) and the bluish green leaves appear succulent. Note the fused stipules forming a sheath around the nodes on the stems.

Pterostegia
Pterostegia drymarioides

Blooms	Plant Height	Flower size	Origin	Life-form
Mar-June	<16 in	Very small	Native	Ann

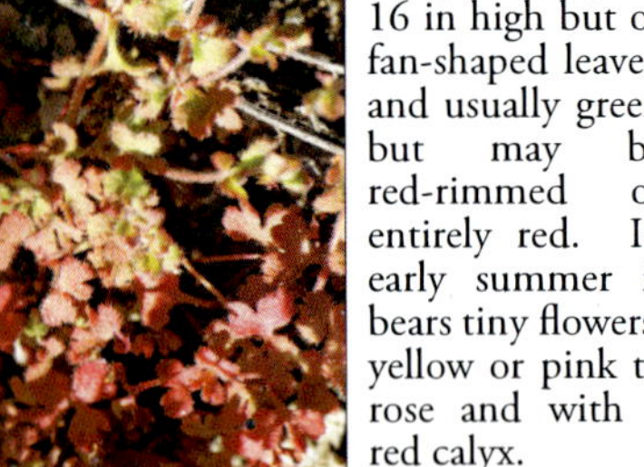

This will be found in grassland or beneath shrubs along the edges of trails. It may grow as much as 16 in high but often appears in a prostrate form. Its fan-shaped leaves, usually in pairs, are slightly hairy and usually green but may be red-rimmed or entirely red. In early summer it bears tiny flowers, yellow or pink to rose and with a red calyx.

Common Purslane
Portulaca olaracea

Blooms	Plant Height	Flower size	Origin	Life-form
May-Sept	2-3 in	Very small	E hemisphere	Ann

Like the Common Knotweed, this has fleshy oval to spoon-shaped leaves and long prostrate, light reddish-brown stems up to 8 in long. Unlike the Knotweeed, the stems are smooth with no sheaths around the nodes. Tiny yellow flowers are borne in mid-summer.